DATE DUE		

The Figure Skating Book

THE
Figure Skating
BOOK

A YOUNG
PERSON'S GUIDE
TO FIGURE SKATING

Debbi Wilkes

FIREFLY BOOKS

A FIREFLY BOOK

Published by Firefly Books Ltd., 1999

First Printing

Library of Congress Cataloguing-in-Publication Data

Wilkes, Debbi,
Figure skating/Debbi Wilkes.

[128 pp] p. ill. ; cm.
Includes index
Summary: Instruction for the most commonly performed maneuvers, accompanied with step-by-step photographs and line drawings.

ISBN 1-55209-444-9 (hc.)
ISBN 1-55209-445-6 (pbk.)
1. Skating. I. Title.
796.91/2   –de21   1999

Published in Canada in 1999 by Key Porter Books Limited.

Published in the United States in 1999 by
Firefly Books (U.S.) Inc.
P.O. Box 1338, Ellicott Station
Buffalo, New York, USA
14205

Electronic formatting: Jean Lightfoot Peters
Design: Peter Maher

Printed and bound in Canada

Contents

The Figure Skating Book

Introduction

So, you want to be a figure skater.

Are you ready for the cold, long hours, early mornings, frustration and thrills?

I knew I could count on you.

There's something intoxicating about skating. It's physical and artistic, and yet there is enough speed and power to make it feel really exhilarating. By learning even the most basic skills you will learn to appreciate, in a whole new way, the talent it takes to be one of the best skaters in the world. Up 'till now, you've been a spectator in a spectator's sport—you've never been fully in on the action. With the help of this book, you won't be watching from the sidelines anymore. This is your invitation to join the party.

Skating is physical freedom. For me, the ability to express my body through movement is like creating a whole new language. Sometimes it's a feeling of oneness with the outside world and sometimes it's a contest: the control of my body against the mighty forces of nature. If I chew ice, I know nature has won once again.

If you really want to be a skater, it's important to know you'll have good days and bad days. Naturally, success will keep you coming back to the rink, but don't be afraid of failure either.

Let's start small. Many of you who have never been on a pair of skates will no doubt appreciate taking things very slowly. Those of you who already have some experience on the ice may feel beyond the status of "beginner," but in doing the research for this book, I made discoveries

by the boot-full, and to an old skater who considers herself an expert, that was a rather humbling experience. Just remember, it's a good idea to read the entire lesson through before starting the steps.

Oh, and by the way, we'll have some fun doing these lessons, too.

See you on the ice!

Chapter 1
Choosing to Skate

The First Step—Buying Equipment

In your quest to become a figure skater, no decision is more important than the one you'll make about buying your equipment.

HOW MUCH TO SPEND

I'm not going to beat around the bush: it's expensive to buy quality boots and blades. For every extra penny you can put toward their purchase, you'll get one hundred times that value in return. With the right skates, your progress will be inspiring; with the wrong skates, you'll soon want to throw them in the closest garbage bin.

If you think about it, you're asking your body to do the most amazing things, even during the simplest of tasks. Without the security and support of top-notch skates appropriate to your level, not only are you risking injury, you're sabotaging the confidence you need to try. If your boot is doing its job, you'll feel safe trying things on one foot. In a poor boot, your aches and disappointments will be so numerous you'll begin to think *you* are the problem. I can't tell you how many times interested beginners have given up in frustration because their "ankles are weak." Phooey! There's no such thing as weak ankles, only weak boots.

I'm not saying you need to spend your inheritance to get started in new boots. I am simply suggesting you choose your boots carefully. Shop around for a perfect fit and for a boot that is strong enough to hold your ankles firmly upright.

SMART SHOPPING

Begin your search by making inquiries at the local skating club and asking for information about retail outlets specializing in skating equipment, either domestically produced or imported. Oh, and by the way, except for very tiny pre-school skates, boots and blades will be bought separately, the blades mounted by a professional recommended by the store.

Check out whether your local skating club has an annual second-hand sale of skates— a dandy place to pick up top-of-the-line equipment. These skates may be a bargain but first make absolutely sure the bargain fits, otherwise your money will be wasted.

If you do decide to purchase second-hand boots, bear in mind that good ones will not look destroyed. They will show signs of wear and tear of course, but the leather (and boots *must* be leather) should still be firm and thick. Make sure you check around the ankle, the lines molded to the shape of the foot of the former owner should be faint, not gouged into the boot.

Usually second-hand boots are sold with the blades already attached. That's OK provided you look closely at how much "life" is left in the blade. At the bottom of every blade, you'll see a dull line running horizontally along the steel, on the side from toe to heel, at a depth of approximately $\frac{1}{16}$th to $\frac{1}{8}$th of an inch from the bottom. If it's anything less than that, or if the blade comes to a thinning point at the heel, it's been through too many wars and may not have enough tempered steel left in it to keep a good sharpening. You should keep looking.

It is also very important to look at the toe picks. Are they intact? Scary as toe picks may seem on the ice, you need them. Picks are to your boots what toes are to your feet—balancing points. If they've been shaved off, it's a good sign some hockey puck has been sharpening those blades. Leave them at the sale.

So What Is a Good Fit?

Professionals suggest trying on many different lines of boots in order to find the style most comfortable for your particular shape of foot. Choose a day when you're feeling well rested and have time to browse and listen carefully to the expert that is fitting you. The salesperson knows the equipment and will take care to direct you to the skate appropriate for your goals. Remember to always wear thin socks when trying on skates and forget about choosing anything that is a size or two too large. That kind of attitude defeats the purpose of spending money on good skates. If the skates don't fit properly, your foot will slip around inside the boot causing blisters at best and huge frustration at worst. Who needs that kind of pain?

When you first put your foot into the boot, you may feel like you're stuck in a cement block. That's a good sign because it means the boot has support and endurance—two of the best things to spend your money on.

Check to see if your foot settles completely along the base of the boot. If you can't feel the flat of your foot softly meeting the boot, if it's too narrow, if your toes are pinched or if the boot crushes any part of your foot, choose a different style. In a properly fitted skate, your toes should be able to wiggle slightly. There should be no movement in the heel at all, and the indentations of the shoe should conform gently to your foot.

The area of the arch is also critical. Some boots are made for people with high arches. There should be no specific force or painful spot anywhere along your arch. If you sense any discomfort now, it's only going to get worse once you move to the ice.

The final test is to move. Tie the laces up loosely and walk around to get a sense of the boot's comfort. Although you'll be clumsy, you'll know when you've hit "pay-dirt."

SKATE GUARDS

The last step is to purchase a suitable pair of skate guards to cover and protect your blades when you're wearing them off the ice. Your skating store will have lots of choices from plain, heavy-duty rubber to guards with funny faces on them. Remember, guards should fit your blades *exactly*. For additional protection during storage, many skaters buy or make blade covers. Made out of toweling, these fuzzy little envelopes are perfectly suited to replace guards while your skates are waiting in your skate bag for their next chance to perform. If you don't have a pair of "fuzzies," don't worry. But do not, under any circumstance, *ever* store your blades with the guards still on. The moisture from the melting snow you accumulate on the ice will cause rust on the bottom of your blades—bad news for blades, but more about that later.

BREAKING IN YOUR SKATES

Once you've made your decision about what kind of skates to buy, and you have the little beauties at home, "breaking in" your skates should be next on the agenda. Try to wear them around the house (with your guards on, of course). Walk up and down the stairs, watch television, do whatever you can. The idea is for your feet to sweat. This process will encourage the leather of your boots to mold to the shape of your foot. Some people speed up the process by wearing warm, damp socks the first few times. Although it feels pretty disgusting, it does a great job.

BLISTERS

Remember, the better the connection of boot to foot, the better the results (and the fewer the blisters!). If blisters do appear, and it's not uncommon, visit your pharmacy and get some "moleskin," a large sheet of flannel with adhesive backing. Cut out a piece that is three times the size of your wound, stick it directly on your skin and leave it there for several days, even when you shower. As you skate, the moleskin will allow the injured area to toughen up, without causing further pain from the boot rubbing against the skin.

The most important thing is not to get discouraged. Breaking in skates takes time. You'll feel bruises and pressure points in places you didn't know existed. Depending how often you wear your new skates, they may take as long as a month to begin to feel really comfortable.

Sharpening and Care

If I could yell this, I would:

Always have your skates sharpened by a reputable figure skating specialist, someone recommended by your equipment store, training center or skating club.

TO SHARPEN OR NOT TO SHARPEN

When done right, a good sharpening will last anywhere from several weeks to several months, depending on how often you skate and how well you look after your blades. It's definitely time to re-sharpen if your blades are slipping or sticking, or not carving forcefully into the ice. (If you're feeling frustrated because skating feels like trying to cut into a piece of meat with a dull knife you probably need a sharpening.) The feeling of the edge as you're moving should be smooth, confident and, above all, easy. You shouldn't have to "work" at it or wonder if your blade is going to hold on to the ice.

Where you skate and on what kind of ice conditions is another factor affecting how often your blades should be sharpened. Normally, skating on well-maintained ice surfaces that are frequently flooded will increase the life span of your sharpening. If, however, just once, you skate outdoors on a natural (and by that I mean unrefrigerated) surface, get thee to a sharpener pronto. Nothing can eat up your blade like dirt, dust and pollution.

Curve of blade

The Mechanics of the Blade

Figure skating blades are unique: they're wider on the bottom than hockey blades, though they have the same inside and outside edges (the inside edge is under your foot's arch, the outside edge is on the outside of the foot, under your baby toe).

What makes a figure skating blade different from a hockey blade is, if you look at the length of your blade, sideways from the toe to the heel, it's more curved and rounded. That's called the "rocker" and, at first, that is what makes you feel tippy and off balance. No wonder you can't stop rocking forward and backward! There's actually very little of your blade touching the ice.

To preserve this delicate shape, you need an experienced sharpener with the right tools. Since sharpening requires special expertise and equipment, never entrust your blades to a hockey sharpener, or worse, to some unmanned machine. Here's why: Each part of the blade is designed for different types of movement. For instance, if some bozo messing with the roundness of the rocker flattens your blade out, you'll never be able to turn backwards on one foot. Why? With a flatter blade, there's too much of the blade on the ice at one time. During the turn, the blade will get caught and stop your rotation.

And please, do not let anyone talk you into shaving off the toe picks. In addition to helping with your balance, you need the toe picks to perform the specific jumps, spins and footwork you're about to learn.

GENERAL SKATE MAINTENANCE

Keeping your skates clean and maintained is an important part of protecting your investment. (After all, you may be able to sell your skates in a second-hand sale at some future time.) The best habit, and one you must acquire, is to look after your blades on a daily basis, and that means keeping them dry between practices.

During the course of a skating session, your blades will pick up lots of snow from the ice. If you ignore the ice build-up when you take your skates off, the edges on the bottom of your blades will become rusty. Rust is a blade's worst nightmare; it destroys the sharpening and reduces the blade's life.

How do you stop rust from developing?

After every use, dry your blades completely with a soft cloth or chamois (you can buy this from any skating supply store), and remember to never store your blades with the guards on. Those guards that you wear to protect your blades walking from the dressing room to the ice surface will collect melted snow and become a breeding ground for rust if you don't remove them while you store your skates. If your blades feel sticky when you step on the ice, that's rust talking. Take more care when drying.

Many skaters will store their boots wrapped in towels or fuzzies in their skating bag to protect them from moisture. This is a great idea. Not only does it give your boots and blades extra protection, but if there is any condensation left on your blades the towels will absorb it.

This may seem like a huge ordeal, but it won't take long to get the routine down to a few minutes and it's certainly worth the extra effort to keep your equipment in first-class shape. You wouldn't think of running a marathon in tattered running shoes, so don't expect your skates to perform unless you take good care of them.

Clothing

In the beginning, put aside your images of Michelle Kwan and Ilia Kulik and how splendid they look on the ice. Right now, settle for "costumes" with a little less glitter, and find some clothes with a lot more practicality. Here's a place you don't need to spend a fortune.

Training clothes should be safe (I recommend helmets for toddlers), comfortable, lightweight, stretchy and warm. Bear in mind that many rinks are not heated, so choose layers that can be easily shed once you've warmed up. On your upper body, put cotton next to your skin (it allows your skin to breathe), maybe a long-sleeved T-shirt, then something a bit heavier, such as a sweatshirt, and finish off with a toasty warm sweater or warm-up jacket.

For women, it's really not necessary to wear one of those precious little skating skirts on your lower body. I find good old sweat pants or heavy leggings offer terrific coverage and have some "give" in the fabric that doesn't restrict movement.

For men, pants are a bit tougher to choose. Sweat pants are always acceptable, but if you can spend a little more money, all the major sports brands sell spandex or lycra jogging pants that are good looking, flexible and warm.

What about wearing jeans? They're losers for two reasons: first, they're freezing in the cold; and second, the fabric is stiff, with no elasticity. In jeans, you'll feel like you're wearing a straightjacket. Leave them at home.

I've already talked about wearing thin socks or tights on your feet. If you're worried about keeping your feet warm, practice harder. As your body warms up, so will your toes. Some skaters prefer to wear nothing on their feet, finding that socks make their feet slip in their boots.

When it comes to wearing gloves, do what feels best. I find some security in wearing gloves. If you fall, the rink can be cold and wet on bare hands—but don't forget that skating is more than pushing across the ice with your feet; it's an expression of movement with the whole body. If your hands are covered, that power of expression may feel dull.

Although these suggestions are merely guidelines, there are a few big no-no's:

- No ski suits—too warm.

- Never tie leftover laces at the boot top around your leg—too dangerous. If the laces are too long, tuck them into the top of the boot.

- Never tuck the bottom of your pants into the tops of your boots—cuts off circulation.

- Never tie your laces too tightly—cuts off circulation and causes cold feet. (A good rule is to tie the lower half of the boot fairly strongly up to your ankle, then loosen gently as you get to the top of the boot, with enough room to be able to insert two fingers side-by-side between the boot's tongue and your lower shin.)

- No scarves—too dangerous and too distracting.

- No hats—reduces visibility. (And gives you "hat head.")

When it comes to clothing, consider all the no-no's, experiment with your gear, and look around at what other skaters are using. I know you'll find the perfect combination of comfort, warmth and style.

Choosing a Club

Learning a new sport can be a thrill a minute. Not only is it a chance to test the body and the mind, it's also an opportunity to make new friends and share in an exciting new hobby that reaches far beyond the ice surface.

There are, however, many questions and potential pitfalls for the misinformed: Should you take skating lessons? If so, how do you find a reputable coach? Where do you train? How do you know if you're getting good value for your money?

Regardless of where you live, the best place to start is at an ice rink. Pay an arena a visit and ask lots of questions about figure skating schedules. Many communities, both large and small, will have

organized skating clubs using the facilities, a fact that will provide you with easy access to both skating programs and coaches.

STEP TWO

Check to make sure the local club is affiliated with a national organization (in Canada, it's the Canadian Figure Skating Association; in the U.S., it's the United States Figure Skating Association) to ensure you are participating in a standardized program with top-level coaches.

STEP THREE

If you live in a large city, you will probably have some other options, too. Phone the Parks and Recreation Department of your municipality for information on "learn-to-skate" programs offered either free-of-charge or for a very nominal fee. Although the level of instruction is generally basic, it's a wonderful way to get started and often provides specialized lessons, too.

STEP FOUR

If you decide to take the route of joining a skating club, and you have more than one choice of club, shop around and compare prices, programs and schedules. Most clubs will allow you a couple of occasions as a "guest" (some for a small fee). Take advantage of it. Sit in the stands, hang around the lobby and talk to the people. You'll get a feeling for the health and vitality of the club based on its members. Is it friendly or competitive? Do you see lots of action on the ice or are skaters spending most of their time draped along the boards? Are people helpful? Since any membership will require a considerable outlay of money, be sure you like what you're seeing and you feel comfortable.

Many of these suggestions may seem like an enormous amount of work, but personally, I think it's worth it. Nobody starts out planning to become a champion or even an expert; this can only happen when a little progress is mixed with a bit of talent and a lot of hard work—it's a dynamite combination.

Choosing a Coach

Finding the right skating club is an important first step for any skater, but no single person will have a greater effect on your progress than your coach will.

Likely, your first personal relationship with a coach will be during group lessons offered as part of your membership fees. It won't be anything like a close friendship and you may not have a choice of coach for group instruction, but it will give you a chance to measure the coach's skills from a couple of different views. Do they appear knowledgeable? Do their students achieve their goals? Does the teaching situation create a desire to learn and practice? Is the atmosphere friendly and encouraging?

Private lessons will be the next step, not essential to the beginner, but after learning the basics in group instruction, they can be a real boost to the speed of a skater's progress. If you have the "bug," a private lesson once a week can really feed your appetite. Ask around before choosing a private coach. Again, look at what's happening out on the ice surface during sessions. Who is having fun?

First Time on the Ice

Yup, it's scary. Ice is cold, slippery and very hard...so take it easy when you start.

When you first step on the ice, you will experience something totally new. You'll probably find that you have no control. If you fall, you may get a few bumps and on a really bad day, a bruise or two. The good news is there are no long-term negative effects from learning to skate.

Before you take your first step, let's work on a few basic ideas that we'll talk about more once your heart rate has returned to normal. Please forgive me if I sound like a broken record, but these few suggestions are so important for your progress, I'll be repeating them throughout the book.

- **Posture and balance** are everything. Despite the fact you're on skates, your posture on the ice is no different from when you're walking down the street. Stand erect. Check that nothing is sticking out—your head, shoulders, hips and feet should be perfectly lined up—and no leaning forward!

- **Bend your knees.** Slightly bent knees will keep you out of a lot of trouble by absorbing the shock of movement. Bent knees act like giant springs; they keep firmness and control in the lower half of your body.

- **Relax your shoulders.** If your knees are doing their job, the upper part of your body can simply go along for the ride. You'll feel comfortable and find movement easy. We'll call it "co-ordination."

- **Carry your hands and arms at waist level.** Unnecessary tension can creep into the upper body by either holding your arms at a level that's too high or by stretching them out too stiffly. Keep your palms facing down, relaxed but not droopy.

At this point, feeling safe and secure is your number one priority.

Many first-timers stick to the boards, clutching them with either one or both hands. This is a bad idea for a couple of reasons. First of all, your upper body is twisted, keeping you off balance. Second, you end up pulling yourself around the rink with your arms instead of pushing yourself with your feet.

If you do feel the need to hang on to something, use a strong chair, like a walker, in front of you. Or ask a "buddy" to lend you some support.

Since the goal of good skating is to move through space free of normal friction, this apparent "lack of control" is actually a glimpse into what makes skating so glorious—freedom!

Walking

STARTING

Take a deep breath. Here we go.

Ever so gently try, either hanging on to a chair in front of you, or if you're brave, without any help, to shuffle your feet along the ice, one foot at a time. Don't break any speed limits—move slowly and carefully from one foot to the other. Just walk.

GLIDING

Almost immediately, you'll become aware that something interesting is happening down where your blades meet the ice. Can you feel it? It's called skating, and your movement may be small, but you're starting to glide. As you move from one foot to the next, the foot you're stepping off of is creating a thrust or "push." For every bit of energy you put into each step by "pushing," the glide from your blades will triple. If you can put more strength and power into each "push," your speed will increase, but don't get too wild just yet.

As you continue your gliding shuffle, run through your checklist to make sure your posture hasn't gone mad. Are you standing straight? Bending your knees? Staying relaxed? Where are your arms and hands? With practice, these four questions will become so ingrained, you won't even have to think about them.

Now that you're under way, what happens next?

In skating, you don't have to keep pushing all the time to keep moving. Take a few steps, and then bring your feet back together, and glide. Try it again. And keep repeating those same few steps . . . and checking your list.

Once you start to glide, don't be surprised if you begin to panic or get so tense, you feel like you've swallowed instant body cement. This is a brand-new feeling and no amount of television watching or rink-side viewing can prepare you for the real thing.

In the beginning, your arms may have a mind of their own, flailing in circles and throwing you out of control. Or your body may want to take you in the opposite direction from your feet. It may also seem like your toe picks are constantly tripping you. Once you get a few laps under your belt though, everything will settle down and in no time you'll begin to understand the feeling. The key is patience, and practice.

STOPPING

There you are, moving along, one step at a time, starting to take note of your posture and carriage and all of a sudden, you see the boards from the other end of the ice coming up fast. A little voice inside your head starts to yell, "What do I do now? Help!!!"

In skating, getting "stopped" is almost as important as getting started.

You have two choices. You can either crash into the boards . . . or learn to stop with your skates. The board-crashing method is effective and you may have no choice but to use it at first, but it can be messy and it's definitely *not* glamorous. Instead, experiment dragging one blade a short distance behind you with the toe turned out and away from the body so that your two blades make an "L" shape. Keep your arms in a neutral position out to the side. Dragging your blade along the ice will create friction and as you continue the action, your blade will gather snow. It's a rather slow stopping action but it works and is fine for now. (We'll cover advanced stopping techniques later on.)

Remember: don't expect too much too soon.

There is another stopping method, of course—falling. Since it'll probably happen to you sooner or later, let's get it out of the way right now.

Falling Down and Getting Up

FALLING

Make friends with the ice.

In any type of skating session, you'll see kids frolicking and sliding, spending more time on their bottoms than upright on their skates. They are not afraid of falling. Unfortunately, the older you get, the larger the fear of falling becomes. In my experience, the only way to combat that is to get down on the ice and roll around on it. In other words, practice falling. Get up some speed and let yourself "plop" and slide.

It may not be a sophisticated tactic, but it's amazing to see how quickly the fear factor drops once you're sliding on the ice. It's hard to be afraid of something you've played with.

There are, however, two kinds of falling. There is *planning* to fall and falling as the result of a mistake—something quite different. Frankly, there aren't any good "splatter" techniques that cover every possible scary situation. In time your skill will improve to the point where you can make instant corrections to avoid most spills, but if it is going to happen, let it. Rarely will you hurt yourself. Because you're in motion, any potential for danger is absorbed by your body as it slides.

GETTING UP

Falling down is easy. It's standing up again that's more of a challenge.

First, get into a sitting position and, using your hands for support, turn over so you're on your hands and knees. Next, raise your upper body so you're only kneeling on both knees. Then gradu-

ally shift your weight to one knee, while at the same time bringing your other foot into a position in front of you, ready to stand. Then, steady your body by pressing down on your bent knee with at least one hand, and then, by straightening both knees, gently lift yourself to a fully upright position ending with both feet together.

This is also a moment when you might find your toe picks coming in quite handy. As you're making the move from kneeling on one knee to standing, jab a few of those picks into the ice if you're feeling shaky. Blades will slide but toe picks will lock on to hold you securely. And away you go.

Chapter 2
Basics

Gliding

If you've just stepped on the ice for the first time, gliding will seem about as difficult as a triple Axel. Not to worry! I'm certain you'll be gliding in fifteen minutes...and the clock's running, so let's get going.

Up to this point, you've mastered walking, balancing and falling and getting up. Next, we're going to try skating by focusing on the parts between the pushes—the glide.

THE GLIDE

The plan is to move in a forward direction in a slightly zig-zaggy pattern. Starting very slowly, try taking a few forceful walking steps and, bringing your feet completely back together after each series of pushes, see if you can glide on two feet for a short distance.

While you're getting that organized, there are three things to think about.

- Make sure you alternate feet on your pushes; otherwise you'll only get better at pushing with one foot.

- Make your movement smooth. Anything jerky can throw you off balance.
- Lastly, relax!

A Good Foot

During performances on television, have you ever heard the announcers talk about a skater having "a good foot"? This is a reference to the skater's ability to glide, how they line up their body to reduce friction and therefore increase speed. No matter what trick is executed, even if it's badly done, a skater with "a good foot" will have the kind of superior body control that will keep the speed consistent and the motion comfortable to watch. These skaters make it look easy. Those with poor glide appear to be skating on sandpaper, their arms waving around and their body moving awkwardly.

ACHIEVING CONTROL

"Control" is a big word on the rink and only happens when the body is firm. If your shoulders have tensed, you're too tight. On the other hand, you don't want your body too loose, either. The key is to skate from the feet up, not from the shoulders down. If your shoulders are tense, all the natural feedback that comes up from the ice to help you balance gets lost. In time, your body will learn to respond and adjust to your movement, however bizarre.

SKATING BACKWARD

The same steps apply to skating backward as they do to skating forward. Begin by taking small steps backward, one foot at a time. This feeling will be considerably more awkward than moving forward, but stick with it. When you push to move forward, your toes naturally turn out and away from the body, with the feet and legs reaching out behind the body. Backward pushing is completely the opposite; during the thrust, which happens in front of the body, the heels push *away* and the toes turn *in*. Although at first everything new will seem like something from outer space, in time it will feel smooth and natural.

Learning to get the greatest speed and distance from a glide is the most important skill you'll acquire in skating, so don't scrimp on practice time.

Stopping

At the moment of stopping, you have to make a choice: slam into the boards, sprawl across the ice, or use one of the official types of stopping techniques by gaining control and learning to skid to a stop using the bottom of your blades—like the L-stop mentioned earlier.

In order of difficulty, the types of stops are the following: the snowplow, the side stop or hockey stop, and the T-stop (a more advanced form of the L-stop). All can be accomplished with a little knowledge of how your body works.

The theory is, while you push down on the ice, the ice is pushing back at you. As you continue to move forward, you must create a greater force in the *opposite* direction of your movement to stop—a "skid" is what it's called in skating—by pressing into the ice and increasing the friction between your blade and the ice.

THE SNOWPLOW STOP

It's not hard to imagine the snowplow stop if you live in a snowy climate like I do. In the snowplow, both heels turn out and both toes turn in, forming an upside-down "V" with your feet. To create the skid, bend your knees so they act like giant springs, lean slightly back, balance around the middle of each blade and concentrate on creating a pressure point in both feet with just enough gentle force to cut the ice and make snow shavings.

THE SIDE STOP

The side stop or hockey stop works the same as the snowplow, the only difference being the feet are in a position side-by-side, parallel to one another and nearly perpendicular to the direction of travel. The body is still facing forward, but both feet have swung 90 degrees. This one is used for stopping quickly.

will come from angling the foot to the outside edge and leaning slightly back over it. If you tilt toward the inside edge, you may "catch" your edge (another unnerving situation where the edge grabs the ice and stops you before you're ready!). Both feet

THE T-STOP

The toughest and the most graceful stop is the T-stop, done either with one foot behind in a "T" position (a back "T") or with one foot in front (a front "T"). To learn these positions, stand facing the boards and hang on with both hands.

With your arms in neutral and looking down at your feet, stand on the left, lift the right foot up and place it on the ice behind the left heel to form a "T" position with the right toe turning to the right. Gently transfer your weight to the right foot. Even standing still, you'll feel the edge of the right blade connecting with the ice. Experiment with the amount of pressure you put on the right foot and with the angle of the foot. The best result

remain on the ice, although when you get really confident, you may lift the left foot completely off the ice.

Try it at slow speed until you get comfortable. Or try to stand slightly away from the boards and then pull yourself closer as you test the T-stop position.

THE FRONT T-STOP

For the front T-stop, begin with the same principle, but lower the right foot in a "T" position in front of the left, still turned out with the toe to the right. Tenderly apply pressure to the outside edge of the right foot.

And you know what...if you stopped within five feet, you could join the chorus line of any ice show. The front T is an old show trick and one of the many requirements for making it through a show audition.

Direction of Rotation

The term "direction of rotation" is confusing, even for experienced skaters. Some people talk about being a "left-to-right jumper," or being a "counter-clockwise spinner." These descriptions are all methods of explaining in which direction a skater feels most comfortable turning.

For the purposes of this book, I will describe jumps and spins that turn in a *counter-clockwise direction* (CCW). (Imagine that you're looking down at the ice surface from the roof of the arena.) Unlike ballet dancers, skaters develop their sense of rotation in only one direction. If a skater is left-handed, it may feel more natural for him or her to spin clockwise. Whatever a skater's preference, their jumps and spins should rotate the same way.

GENERAL NOTES

Every skater, beginner or expert, will instinctively feel a preference for rotating either to the right—clockwise (CW) or to the left—counter-clockwise (CCW). To find out which is best for you, you don't even have to be on skates. Stand on the floor and give yourself a push in either direction. Try turning first one way, then the other. Whichever direction feels more comfortable (likely the one you tried first), is your natural direction of rotation.

Reverse Jumpers

Back in the old days, coaches would go to great lengths to discourage students from developing clockwise (CW) rotation. I shudder to think how many potentially great skaters were turned off of skating because they couldn't conform. Today, thankfully, athletes who were once called "reverse jumpers," because of their preference for CW rotation, are much more common and accepted.

Forward Edges

I was trained to believe that every aspect of skating is inter-connected. Free skating, dancing and figures are so closely related, in fact, that when you learn one skill, it expands to include movement in all other disciplines. A good back outside edge on a figure "8," for example, is the same back outside edge on a jump landing. Being a rather lazy skater, I like that idea. Why learn it more than once?

There are four basic edges—forward outside, forward inside, backward outside and backward inside. These four edges and their combinations are the building blocks of every major skating element.

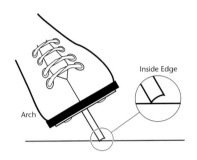

STEP ONE

Start by standing on one foot at the boards to give yourself some extra balance. Tilt the "skating foot," that's the one you're on, by pressing it ever so slightly in the direction of your baby toe. Try the same thing on the other foot. In each case, as your balance shifts to the outside of your foot, you move to the outside edge.

STEP TWO

Still at the boards, try tilting your foot in the other direction for an inside edge, toward your arch and big toe.

STEP THREE

Once you understand steps one and two, try the same shifting-of-balance sequence while moving away from the boards. Instead of skating in straight lines, glide on two feet on one of the hockey circles in the rink and continue practicing, curving gently in either direction. Every so often lift one foot and increase the length of those glides depending on your level of comfort. Be careful. Make sure you devote an equal amount of time and practice to both directions; otherwise you'll find yourself improving in one direction only.

STEP FOUR

Next, put it in motion on one foot with a harder push beginning in a straight line, keeping your back erect and skating with knees bent. Moving counterclockwise (CCW), begin to press your left boot slightly to the outside of your left foot, toward your baby toe, for an outside edge, or toward your big toe on your right foot for an inside edge. If you find yourself curving, you're doing "edges"!

For a deeper or curlier shape, press a little harder, but if you curve too tightly, you'll probably want to put the other foot, the "free" foot, down on the ice for balance. That's OK. It's there to help you stay out of trouble.

STEP FIVE

To get more control while you're moving, think about tucking the free foot in slightly behind the skating foot, but keep concentrating on holding your shoulders fairly level with the ice and your arms at waist level at your sides. You may sense a whipping feeling because you've let your body twist out of shape or you're swinging your arms around yourself. Check to see if your posture is still good or if your hips are sticking out in funny directions. When you get them back underneath you, everything gets much easier.

STEP SIX

Now let's put a set of curving edges together. Imagine a line across the width of the rink, or use one of the existing hockey lines, if you like. Starting at one side, skate your edges first on one foot and then on the other, making curves or arcs alternating on each side of the line all the way across the ice.

GENERAL NOTES

Eventually you'll feel you can make the size of your edges larger until they are perfectly shaped half circles. Start them as tiny curves and increase their size until you can skate them with a width approximately three times your height. The goal here is to be able to glide on one curve... forever. It's a magnificent sensation and probably the first time you'll feel like you're really skating. It's like flying!

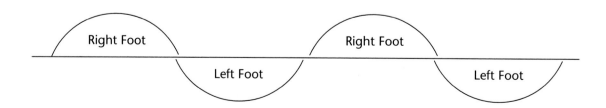

Backward Edges

Just like the forward edges, learn-ing to skate edges backward can begin with some simple exercises to get yourself ready.

STEP ONE

To warm up, skate backwards gliding on two feet in the shape of a large circle. Using lots of knee bend, go slowly and care-fully, enjoying the glide between pushes and feeling the natural position of your body. If you're gliding in a counter-clockwise direction, you'll only be pushing, or as skaters call it, pumping, with the left foot, then gliding with the feet together. You will very likely feel that the right arm wants to move behind you with the left arm naturally moving in front. Your shoulders will turn slightly toward the center of the circle and, in order to see where you're going, your head will look in that direction, too.

When you glide, your skates will be moving around the rim of the circle and your shoulders and upper body will be traveling on the same line, right hand leading the circle, left hand following. Is this happening? Good! This is all going exactly as it should.

STEP TWO

Once your comfort level goes up, after the left foot pushes off, lift it slowly off the ice so all your weight moves completely to the right foot. To skate on the outside edge, tilt your boot slightly to the outside of the right foot, but just a bit. See how long you can hold your balance on one foot, then do it again, holding it a little longer each time. Try this ten or twenty times in a row. Then take a breather and start the next step. For an inside edge, pump with the left foot, then glide on it and lift the right foot up off the ice.

STEP THREE

Ready to try it in the other direction? Clockwise, this time pumping with the right foot, let the left arm lead your movement on the circle with your head looking over the left shoulder. Push... and glide... on the left foot for an outside edge, on the right foot for an inside.

STEP FOUR

Once you feel like it's making sense, and don't rush yourself, here's the next step. Begin at the side of the rink standing on one of the hockey lines crossing the ice surface. See if you can alternate circle shapes, first pushing with the left, then bringing your feet back together and slowly pushing with the right as your curve comes back to the line. Your goal is the same as when you learned your forward edges. Bend your edges around the hockey line, using it like an axis, first in one direction and then in the other, making your way across the width of the rink. At first you may want to skate this pattern of alternating curves on two feet. Go for it. When you're ready, start lifting the pushing foot up even if it's just for a couple of seconds. That's how it all begins.

If you're getting the hang of being on one foot, don't worry too much at this stage about where your free foot (the one not on the ice) should go. For now, just keep it crossed over in front of your skating foot with some pressure on it, close to the ice so it won't go flying around like a flag in a wind storm. You will sense the arms and body wanting to turn. That's OK, but if you do feel out of control, just put the free foot back down on the ice until you've recovered your balance.

Little by little, your skill and control will improve and the distance you can glide will increase until the sizes of your curves approach full half circles.

GENERAL NOTES

If you're getting frustrated and progress seems to be a figment of your imagination, trouble-shoot with the following checklist.

How's your posture? Are you standing up straight?

Are you sticking your hips out? That makes for some craziness.

When you push, are you scratching up on your toe picks? Your weight should be somewhere around the ball of the foot (the lumpy section just behind your toes). A good trick to use to find the perfect balance point is to bounce gently while you're gliding. The body will automatically correct itself.

Is your body stiffening up? If rigor mortis has set in, you're in trouble. Keep the body firm but relaxed.

Forward Stroking

"Stroking" is a general term used by skaters to describe the whole series of pushes and glides needed to cover one full circuit of the rink. It consists of two types of steps; one for traveling in a straight line down the sides of the rink, which we'll tackle first, and one special type of step for going around the corners (we'll cover this later in **Turning Corners**).

You'll find straight line stroking is actually glorified pushing and gliding done with more speed and confidence (and a little more "attitude"). Nothing has changed as far as posture and technique are concerned, but this time, instead of gliding with two feet together, after each push you're going to concentrate on gliding on *one foot* and on stretching the other leg behind.

THE EDGES

Before you get moving, we need to begin your education about those edges on the bottom of your blades and how they're used during stroking. (Remember, the outside edge is the one on the outside of your foot under your baby toe and the inside edge is the one under your arch.)

Each time you stroke (take a look at your feet), you're pushing with the *inside* edge. You'll notice that as you build up the force in your foot to begin each push, the foot will bend slightly in toward the arch, creating a thrust with the inside edge. Since the width of the blade is so narrow, you'll note it takes very little movement or adjustment in the foot to go from an inside edge to an outside edge. So no crazies just yet.

STEP ONE

Let's call the foot you're gliding on your "skating foot," the foot that is actually in touch with the ice. The other foot, the one free of the ice, we'll call your "free foot." (These definitions also apply for other parts of the body; e.g., the "free side" is the same side of the body as the "free foot.") Of course, with every push or thrust, your skating foot will alternate from right to left to right, and so on. Between each push, be sure to bring your feet completely back together.

STEP TWO

Your toe picks should never be used when stroking forward. To avoid this, as you build up the force and push, bend your knees and gently turn the pushing toe out and away from the body so your stroke moves on an angle

halfway between your side and your back. Keep in mind, the more you bend your knees, the stronger and more powerful your stroke will be. When your push reaches its limit and leaves the ice, stretch your free leg behind and hold it there for several seconds before bringing it back on to the ice beside the other foot. For a brief moment, you'll be gliding on two feet, then simply repeat the action in the other direction pushing with the other foot.

STEP THREE

After each thrust, you need to find somewhere to place that foot and leg that is comfortable. That foot helps you to keep your good form and maintain your speed. To find that special spot, stand at the boards on two feet and imagine a fat, straight line coming off the back of your blades. Holding one foot about three or four inches above the ice, stretch your free leg behind until your free foot is somewhere over that imaginary line. If you need to, look again! Once your foot has found the spot and your free leg is fully extended, turn your toe out and point it until

your instep or arch is facing the ice. Memorize that position, and focus on how it feels in your body.

GENERAL NOTES

This may seem kind of spooky, but your goal from here to the end of this book is to develop, without looking, a feeling for when the body is in the right

position. That extra sense will take you a long way. Whether it's with plain stroking or with jumps and spins, when you're feeling uncomfortable, that is a sign that your body's trying to tell you, "You've got me in the wrong place!"

Not needing to look also makes perfect sense if you consider that once you're moving, unless you enjoy smacking into other skaters, you won't want your head and eyes looking anywhere but straight ahead, doing traffic control as it were.

Good Stroking

In all good skating, but particularly with good stroking, try to keep most of the body's movement happening from the waist down, as you move from one step to the next. Pretend you're sitting in the stands at ice level, but behind the boards so you can only see the top half of a skater's body. If you're watching quality stroking, the movement will be so smooth and calm, you won't be able to tell when the skater is actually pushing! That's another reason the knees are so important; when used correctly they soften the sharpness of the effort and absorb harsh movement. Many of today's greatest skaters haven't learned this basic rule and as a result have horrible stroking.

Backward Stroking

I've always found backward stroking easier and more comfortable than forward stroking. The muscles seem to know where to go without being told. When you can sit on an edge and enjoy the flow, your body is more relaxed, your co-ordination feels easier and therefore your sense is that you are "in control."

The first time you skate backward, you'll begin to understand why you have toe picks...and you'll learn to love them! Once moving, they tell you exactly where on the blade is the perfect place to balance. If you're leaning too far forward over your picks, they'll scratch the ice and make a fair amount of noise—that gives you useful information without causing bodily harm. If you're heading backward toward a dangerous situation, your toe picks can be used as instant emergency brakes.

Like stroking forward, good backward stroking concentrates on using deep knee bends while at the same time consulting your posture checklist. Both directions also use an inside edge to power the push. It's their differences, however, that make forward and backward movement so distinctive.

The backward stroking action and the position of the free leg once it's extended is completely reversed from the forward movement. To stroke backwards, everything happens in front of you; the thrust begins by turning the heel of the pushing foot out and away from the other foot in a "C" pattern, and once the "C" push is completed, the free foot is stretched in front.

If it seems confusing, think for a minute about what happens when you walk forward and compare that to what happens if you walk backward. Can you feel the difference? Whether you're moving forward or backward, the direction of your push is *opposite* to the direction in which you want to travel.

STEP ONE

Let's begin once again by standing at the boards but holding on with only one hand and facing sideways. This time, to find where to position your free foot after pushing, place your imaginary line in front of you coming off your toe picks. Try out the action by alternating feet, lifting one foot a few inches off the ice, stretching your free leg and pointing your toe. Each time, hold the position for several seconds, then bring your feet closely back together and lift the other foot in the same manner.

STEP TWO

Now, step away from the boards and try to get moving. Getting the momentum started is the tricky part.

To get rolling, bend your knees and stand with most of your weight on your right foot. Turn your left foot so that the toe is turned in and the heel turned out (like the Snowplow Stop position). Without pressing too hard, let the heel of the left foot push slightly to the side, to make a shape like the top of a "C." Pushing the ice away from you, make it a gentle and continuous movement as you draw the rest of the "C" on the ice, and pull the left heel back in, towards your imaginary line. When you hit it, lift the left foot and leg several inches off the ice, extend and point for several moments. When you're ready, bring your feet back together, transferring your weight from the right to the left to try your "C" in the other direction.

It will probably feel quite awkward at first, but once you get underway with a few strokes, the speed, balance and rhythm will become more obvious.

Speed

It's funny, but in skating everything is much easier to do if you're traveling at moderate speed—not freeway limits—just at a speed fast enough to accentuate and enhance the natural feeling of the movement (a tip to remember when elements get a little tougher).

Turning Corners—Forward and Backward Crosscuts

Stroking in a straight line down the sides of the rink by alternating pushes and glides will get you only halfway around the ice surface. The other half of the problem is learning to travel around the corners—with movements called "crossovers" or "crosscuts." Crosscuts are used everywhere in skating: as warmups, in connecting steps, for spin and jump preparation and in dancing. When I see stroking and crosscuts that are really well done—and that's quite rare—it's exquisite!

FRONT CROSSCUTS

STEP ONE

Again, to get the idea, and this works for both forward and backward crosscuts, stand at the boards and experiment with how it feels to cross one foot in front of the other. The upper part of the legs should be touching so that, if you're crossing the right foot over the left, the back of the right thigh will be gently pressing against the front of the left thigh.

STEP TWO

Begin your practice moving forward by standing on one of the
large hockey circles and traveling
in a CCW direction curving
with the circle. Pushing with the
right foot and gliding on the left
(1), lift the right foot in front,
over the left foot (2). As the right
is crossing over, transfer your
weight to it (3), letting the left
foot push under the right (4).

To explain the motion further,
let's talk about which edges
you're using. Remember, when
you're pushing and gliding in a
straight line, each push is done
with the *inside* edge. In crosscuts,
the foot doing the crossover is
also pushing with the inside
edge, but the foot crossing under,
uses the outside edge. Take a
moment to think about it.

STEP THREE

Each sequence of two pushes—the right and the left—make one crosscut. Combine several cross-cuts, one after the other, crossing the right foot over and the left foot under, and you'll find yourself completely around the circle.

GENERAL NOTES

Extra hints for success:

- Face forward.

- Hold your arms at a comfortable height between your shoulders and your waist.

- In a CCW direction, lead with the right arm and let the left arm move slightly behind you.

- Keep your shoulders evenly balanced and parallel with the ice.

- Lean the body in toward the center of the circle. (The greater your speed, the deeper your lean.)

- Try not to lean forward or "break" at the waist.

- Use deep knee bends for balance and control.

- Place the right foot down on the ice so the blade is traveling along the circle line.

The principle is exactly the same when you're moving CCW backward but with a few alterations in body position. In fact, with time, you'll probably find you prefer the ease and power of back crosscuts over crosscuts moving forward.

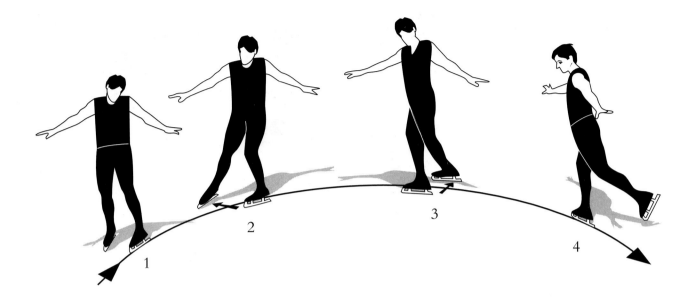

BACK CROSSCUTS

- Face backward.

- Hold the left arm behind to lead the circle and let the right arm move in front of your body (1).

- Since you're traveling backward, face your head into the center of the circle and slightly over your left shoulder.

- Push with the right and step on the left (2).

- Cross the right foot over the left and step on it as the left foot pushes underneath (3) (4).

- After each crosscut, begin the next one by reaching wide with the left foot into the circle and transferring the balance from left to right.

Chapter 3
Simple Turns

Flats and Changes

Before we launch into some of
the simpler turns, it's important
to get a better understanding of
the bottom of your blades.

BACKGROUND

Whoever thought about how to
engineer two edges of steel for a
variety of movements was brilliant, so brilliant in fact that for
decades any major changes or
improvements have been unnecessary. And when you consider
how drastically figure skating has
evolved, the perfect design of the
figure skating blade is a miracle.

Generally speaking, for most skating movement, the back part of the blade is used for skating forward, and the front part of the blade is used for skating backward. Those little gems, the toe picks, help with balance and with specialized moves like jumps and spins. For turning, depending on your direction of movement, your balance rolls back and forth, up and down the rocker of the blade using one edge at a time. That's why a good sharpening is so important. If the edges are nicked, rusty or worn down, the blade can't do the job it was designed for.

Each of your skate's edges will carve out a line or tracing in the ice. If you're gliding in a straight line, you're skating on both edges at the same time on what is called a "flat." Try it for a few feet and then get down on the ice, on your hands and knees, and search for the tracing mark left by your skate. It will look like two faint lines running parallel to one another, separated by a distance the width of your blade.

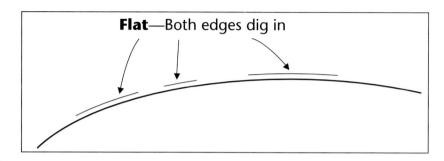

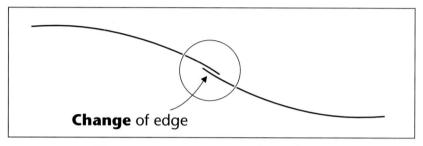

Two common types of tracings

As long as you're traveling in a straight line, a flat is perfectly acceptable; however, once you're moving on a curve, it's a different story. Technically, only one line or edge should be visible on the ice. If a second line, a flat, appears on the tracing, it's a bad thing and indicates poor control and lack of balance—so we'll have to have less of that.

Another picture you can draw on the ice with your blades is called a "change": an "S" shaped edge on one foot. In the middle of the "S" where the curve changes direction is the point on the ice where the edge changes

from outside to inside, or inside to outside. A change can wear two different faces, a happy one if a particular change is planned in the choreography, or a sad face if the change occurs at the wrong moment during an element, again a sign of balance gone crazy.

WHAT DOES A CHANGE LOOK LIKE?

On fresh ice, perform any kind of snaky line, either backward or forward, and then, without stepping over the area, have a close peek at the points where the

Edge Mechanics

Take a closer look at your skate by turning it upside down, with the bottom of the blade facing the ceiling. Hold the boot at eye level. Scanning from heel to toe, check and see how the inside and outside edges are separated by a tiny valley or hollow. Gently run your finger down the length of the blade. (Remember—those blades are sharp!) Are the edges smooth? Can you feel the hollow? The deeper the hollow, the sharper the edges.

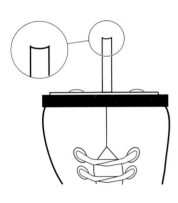

curves shift from one lobe to the other. You'll see one line coming up to the point of the shift, then a second line will join it for a few inches (like a flat), then the first line will disappear leaving the second line alone as the shape curves the other way.

Here's what happened. You skated the first lobe on an outside edge to form a tracing of one line. As your weight started to shift to the other curve, your balance moved from the outside of your foot to the inside of your foot over the arch, creating a moment when both edges made contact with the ice (a flat). In order to skate the other lobe, your weight continued to transfer until it was completely over the inside edge leaving a tracing of one line once again. This movement was a "change of edge" or "change." Simply put, the foot rolled sideways from one edge, to a flat, to the other edge. If you did the sideways roll slowly enough (and concentrated very hard), you would feel the moment when the flat hit the ice (it will make a tiny "thump").

Flats and changes may seem like a bunch of fun and they're great words to throw around at your next skating party, but I want to be very clear here. Unwanted flats and changes are the bad guys when it comes to skating quality turns and edges. Generally in skating you're trying to draw an edge that has only one consistently dark line. No flats or changes. If you make it, that turn or edge is called "clean"... and you'll be wanting lots of those! Figures used to provide the opportunity to really study clean turns and edges, although now, with figures a thing of the past, the "clean edge police" have had to find new jobs. It's not as common these days to see judges and skaters searching the ice closely for clean turns. Still, a good turn has a certain look. It appears easy and comfortable to watch, skated with beautiful form, consistent speed and tons of control.

And the nicest thing is, once you've labored through the mistakes causing flats and changes, you'll discover the easiest turn or edge is the "clean" one.

Three Turns

You're feeling pretty good moving forward and backward, right? Our challenge now is to put those two things together by learning how to *turn* from forward to backward.

Our project in this lesson is to skate a "three turn," named after the number "3" because that's the shape your tracing will draw on the ice. This basic one-footed turn can be done either forward or backward and on inside or outside edges. Considered to be the simplest of the "threes," you're going to tackle the forward inside three (FI3): forward because of your starting direction, and inside due to your starting edge.

Now don't scrunch up your feet or your face; it's not that hard, and we'll begin by trying a few basic things on two feet first... and standing at the boards.

Coming out of a three turn

STEP ONE

First, let's do some prep work. With your feet side-by-side, point them toward one end of the rink, then turn them half a circle to point toward the other end while you keep hanging on to the boards. If you started with your toes pointing to your right, you'll end up with them pointing to your left. Notice that all the rotation is done under the shoulders; for example, you were facing the boards poised over the left hip when you began, but after you turned your feet, you finished facing over the right hip. To say it another way, you're winding up the upper half of your body opposite to the lower half, building up pressure on the ice before you turn your feet. The actual turn occurs at the moment when the pressure of the wind-up is released; the shoulders reverse at exactly the same time as the feet come around. If you were moving, you would have turned from front to back. Try it again, this time starting in the other direction. And again.

STEP TWO

If you feel like you've got the hang of the two-footed movement at the boards, try it on one foot, keeping the free foot and free leg securely behind the skating foot on both sides of the turn, coming in and going out. To do this, hold your knees together so they are gently touching and extend the lower half of your free leg behind. Think of your lower body from your waist to your blade as a unit. The hips cannot change position unless the skate does.

STEP THREE

Stop and think about what it will feel like once you get some momentum and remember, when you're gliding, it creates another important element to control. Every force becomes exaggerated with speed, so when you do move out on to the ice with some flow, just take it a little at a time. Try the two-footed turn on a curve first, then gradually work up to one foot as your balance and confidence improve.

STEP FOUR

Moving away from the boards and using the painted hockey circle as a guideline, skate some of those crosscuts you've been working so hard on and get up some speed. Glide on two feet, feet together, skating on a slight curve. By rotating your shoulders to face into the center of the circle, you'll begin to sense a certain build-up of momentum from the rotation that will help you turn backward. This "wind-up" is the force you're going to harness for the three turn.

STEP FIVE

Ready to try it on one foot?

On the right forward inside edge (RFI) and skating in a CCW direction, move your right arm and right shoulder in front and your left arm and left shoulder behind, winding up your whole upper body to face into the center of the circle. Although you'll find it hard at first not to let your hips (and everything else!) swing too, remember, you're treating the lower body right down to your skate as a unit. No moving the hips without moving the skate. During the shoulder wind-up, it's important to keep that lower unit facing straight forward over your skating foot.

Hold that position, then after a few seconds, release the hold and turn your foot and lower body backward by gently bouncing on the skating knee and bringing the heel of your skating foot around. At the same moment your foot turns, do your washing machine thing by reversing your arms and shoulders so that now you're still facing the center of the circle but with your right arm behind and your left arm in front.

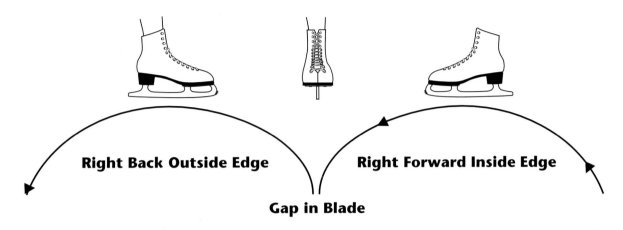

Right Back Outside Edge

Right Forward Inside Edge

Gap in Blade

STEP SIX

During the three, you'll feel your balance change on the blade. The moment you turn backward, your weight will move from the middle of your blade to just behind your picks and, in fact, you may feel the picks scratch the ice as you glide out of the turn backward. Although a good turn should be almost silent, those picks can come in handy during emergencies.

When you're satisfied you've done a good turn, take a close look at the tracing. It should be shaped like a long "3," with one line or edge coming in forward to shape the first curve and another single line exiting backward to make the second curve.

The point where the two curvy bumps touch in the middle of the "3" is where you turned backwards and changed from a forward inside edge to a backward outside edge. If you look more closely at that spot, you'll see a tiny gap in the tracing. That gap is the width of your blade, visible as you tip from forward inside to backward outside.

GENERAL NOTES

A good three turn will have consistent speed, a clean sound with no scratchiness, jumping or skidding, and you'll feel comfortable and capable of gliding for a few seconds after the turn without having to put your free foot down on the ice to regain your balance.

Give the other threes a try: forward outside, backward outside and backward inside. The principles and techniques are all the same, each one with their own quirky little feelings that, if you keep to the basic rules, you'll easily sort out.

Inside Mohawks

Just for fun, let's try something silly.

Skate a few slow forward strokes, then see what you need to do to turn backwards. Bumble through it if necessary. Use both feet, one at a time, and see what happens.

. . .

You probably scared yourself, but without realizing it, you tried a "mohawk," the technical skating name for the most common skating turn.

Background

An inside "mohawk" is a turn from front to back, done on inside edges from one foot to the other foot, on one curve. Where the three turn stays on one foot and changes edges, the mohawk stays on the same edge and changes feet.

Mohawks can be done without thinking. They can be performed with great precision, like a step in ice dancing, or they can be done hockey-style, racing down the rink backwards with no regard for technique or grace. If that works for you, go for it.

If you tried it at the beginning of the section, you were doing a hockey-style mohawk. So now let's get technical and talk about what actually happens if you take it more seriously.

STEP ONE

Skate on the same hockey circle you used for the three turn. Gliding on your left foot but with your right foot still off the ice (1), make a "T" shape with your feet (2). Bring your right free foot halfway along your skating foot, with the free foot turning out so the right heel is against the left arch.

STEP TWO

At this point, you will feel a natural turning in the upper part of the body as the left arm and left shoulder begin to want to move in front. This action is exactly what you need to turn backward, so enjoy the movement and face into the center of the circle. When your shoulders have turned as far as they can go, that's the moment when two things have to happen at the same time: reverse your shoulders like in the three turn, and change feet to glide backward on the right back inside edge (3). Stretch the left foot and leg behind.

STEP THREE

Make sure to try a mohawk starting on the right inside edge, too, moving in a CCW direction. Since everyone prefers to turn one way over another, it's perfectly natural to practice only in the more comfortable direction—but that's a big mistake. A great way to avoid that kind of dilemma is to start your practice session with the mohawk that feels the hardest to control. Since all skaters tend to spend more time on the first thing they try, in no time your poorer element will have improved so much, you won't be able to remember which one you liked better.

Chapter 4
Jumps

Two-Foot Jump

If you have a tendency to get air sick when you think about both feet being off the ice at the same time, maybe you should continue practicing your stroking for a while and let the daredevils throw themselves into the air around you.

No, wait a minute. Part of the thrill of skating is the risk, believing that as your skill develops you will want to set your sights higher. Remember when you started? You couldn't imagine skating backward. You've made BIG progress on the ice and now it's time to see if your new-found body awareness can still be found, even in the air.

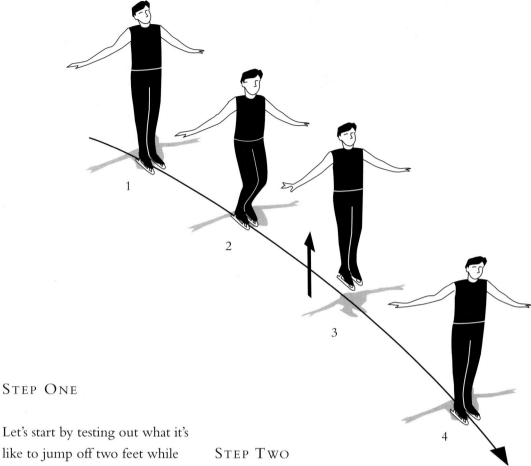

1

2

3

4

STEP ONE

Let's start by testing out what it's like to jump off two feet while standing still. You can hang on to the boards if you need reassurance. This step may seem silly, but think for a moment about two unpredictable things: slippery ice and curved blades. You may be extremely athletic and quick to catch on, but believe me, until you've tamed "the slipperies," you'll be glad you were patient and took this first step. The whole idea about learning to skate is learning to understand what the body feels like when you successfully conquer outside forces.

STEP TWO

All the same balance and form rules apply to the body in the air, as on the ice: standing up straight, looking forward with your head up, arms at waist level, knees softly bent. On spot, try small hops first, concentrating on the feeling during take-off and landing. Then, when you feel brave, begin to move slowly forward and try it once again (1). Once you have even a bit of flow, watch to keep your feet together directly underneath you (2) and spring straight up into

the air by gently hopping off both feet at the same time (3). No rotation is necessary so don't try for some mega jump. Be satisfied with something little—you still have to be able to control the force of the landing.

Step Three

When you do come back down to earth, or ice, land forward on two feet with your knees bent (4). The tendency to bend at the waist will be huge, but that's also what will throw you off balance. It's a big plus if you can think about keeping your back erect.

Step Four

A little faster and a little higher? Oh, and by the way, if you're going to be ready to move on to the next section, the backward toe jump, you'd better practice the two-foot jump backward.

Backward Toe Jump

Skating the two-foot jump backward will probably seem goofy at first. But you must realize that since five out of the six basic jump elements begin from a backward edge, this exercise is an important piece of homework. In addition, the toe picking movement gives you the first chance you've had to really put the picks to work...legally.

STEP ONE

Although jumps are generally performed on a large circle, skating on curves tends to cause a swinging motion in the body that's hard to control for someone learning a new "trick." For the backward toe jump, travel in a straight line and learn the most important aspect of the jump— how to find the perfect spot to place the pick. Once that detail is cemented in your brain, the next step is to move the jump back on the curve and to experiment with the new feeling.

STEP TWO

Rev up your engine traveling backward on two feet in a straight line.

Keeping your knees bent, move all your weight over to the left foot and reach behind with your right leg. Don't worry about whether your right leg is straight or whether you're reaching far enough; about a foot is great. Pointing down with your right toe, place your pick in the ice behind your body in a spot directly in line with your skating foot. Before you jump, I want you to try and transfer your weight to the pick, at the same time bringing your feet as close together as possible (the left foot

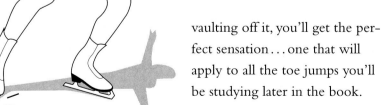

crossed in front of the right would be perfect) and jumping off the toe pick from a bent knee.

To give you an example of the action you're going for, imagine a pole-vaulter as he digs the pole vault into the ground and climbs aboard. If you treat your pick like the pole, transferring your weight to the picking foot and

vaulting off it, you'll get the perfect sensation...one that will apply to all the toe jumps you'll be studying later in the book.

STEP THREE

Your first jump will likely be nothing more than a hiccup, and that's good, because you need to get back down on the ice to land on one foot—your right foot. Notice that your picking foot and landing foot are the same.

STEP SIX

Once up in the air, you'll have to transfer your weight back over the right foot to prepare for the landing, something easy to do if you think about it and plan for it before you leave the ice.

GENERAL NOTES

Are you getting a feeling for the slightly different movements?

Like their unique names, every element in skating has its own special set of sensations. Keep trying new things and making progress and you'll get to know them all.

STEP FOUR

To glide on the landing, stretch your left free leg behind in the forward stroking position. Pay special attention here. Since this is *the* landing position for the most common jumps, you'll be repeating it thousands of times over your skating career. Take the time to get it right. A solid and comfortable landing position can make a crummy jump look ten times better. Except in special circumstances, your right foot will always be your landing foot, but your right toe may not always be the picking foot.

STEP FIVE

Let's change that picking foot and see what happens. The jumping and picking action will be the same, but to land, you'll need to switch feet and settle to the ice on the right. Skate the same setup as the previous manoeuvre, only this time glide backward on your right foot and stretch the left toe back. Line up your pick in the same way as before and when you place it in the ice, move all your weight to it . . . and jump.

Bunny Hop

Let's take a moment and review.

BACKGROUND

The bunny hop is based on the same principles as the two-foot jump except that this time you'll be jumping off one foot. Good form and lots of knee bend are the keys here. And remember to keep your back from tilting forward. Everything becomes much easier if you're standing straight.

I'm going to make some assumptions here. If you're ready to work on the bunny hop, you should be feeling fairly confident about the two-foot jump having worked not only on staying standing throughout, but on increasing your speed and distance across the ice.

Let's skate through the bunny hop in steps. Once again, go back to the boards to experiment with the bunny hop action.

STEP ONE

Stand on your left foot with your right leg held back behind you.

STEP TWO

With gusto, swing your right leg straightforward like a pendulum and as it passes your left leg, JUMP. (Your goal is to do one big running step from left to right, so plan ahead. Think before you jump that your weight will transfer from the left foot to the right.)

STEP THREE

Land on your right toe pick and quickly step onto the left foot (it's a "peg leg" kind of action), pushing with the right toe and then stretching the right leg behind you.

STEP FOUR

Once you have the foot mechanics and jump rhythm clear in your mind, start putting some glide into the action. Arm movement will also help with the comfort of the jump. Begin by pushing on to the left foot with the right arm in front. When the right foot swings in front to jump, change arms so the left is in front; then when the right toe pushes you once again on to the left foot, finish with the right arm in front. This arm feeling, though it sounds complicated, will feel natural once the jump is underway.

GENERAL NOTES

A good bunny hop can be a terrific speed-getter, and with this simple toe jump, you can now begin to understand another reason why toe picks are so important. Once you've got the action down, start putting sequences of bunny hops together so that the landing of the first jump is the take-off of the second one. Lo and behold! You've just done your first jump combination.

Three Jump

Have you been working on your bunny hop?

If you're feeling pretty good about it and your panic attacks are under control, let's get daring. I know jumping is the scariest of all the single elements, but I think you're ready.

STEP ONE

First I want you to glide forward on two feet in a straight line so we can review the two-foot jump. Keeping your posture erect without leaning forward, bend your knees and jump straight up in the air, landing forward on two feet with your knees flexed. You don't have to jump so high you bump your head on the arena rafters, just bounce enough to give yourself some confidence about having both feet up in the air. It only takes a second and you'll be back safely on the ice...still gliding, I hope!

STEP TWO

Next, let's add another wrinkle to the two-foot jump. Try the same thing only backward this time, on two feet and in a straight line. With your experience, I bet you feel more comfortable in that direction now. Notice how the toe picks really help you balance—but remember, you shouldn't scratch too much or your flow will stop. Your picks should only whisper as they touch the ice. More than that and you're using them as brakes. Flow and glide will help make the action work but not necessarily at highway speeds, just fast enough to give yourself

4　　　　3　　　　2　　　　1

Three Jump on One Foot

some momentum. Believe it or not, it's easier with speed. These elements are meant to be done traveling across the ice; otherwise take your skates off and go bounce in the corner.

STEP THREE

Now we're going to put those two exercises together. Think of skating the same pattern as a three turn, but at the point where you would turn backward in the three turn, for the three jump you'll do the turn up in the air instead of on the ice. Start forward on two feet and get your pattern to curve slightly to the left (CCW). Concentrating on form as you prepare to jump (1), anticipate turning your shoulders and head one-half rotation to the left, in the same direction as your curve (2). Start your jump and before you touch down, turn your feet and body so that they land backward (3). This may seem like a lot of extra movement but if you can, hang on. Bending those knees deeply and keeping your back straight will help you stay in control (4).

Holding your arms out at your side will also give you further support... Still breathing? Congratulations! You've just completed your first half rotation jump. This is the big time.

STEP FOUR

Even bigger is how you're going to feel when you do the same exercise on *one* foot, from a left forward outside edge to a backward inside edge on the same foot. I must emphasize that the take-off forward and the landing backward happen without changing feet.

GENERAL NOTES

What are some of the problems you might face in getting a good three jump completed?

Skidding the take-off is a very common nuisance caused by starting the rotation before leaving the ice.

Maybe you can't get yourself to turn the full half rotation? By stiffening up on the take-off, you can't take advantage of the jumping and turning action you've set up by skating on the curve.

Waltz Jump

There is some confusion in the skating world between the three jump and the waltz jump— another half rotation jump. The take-offs are exactly the same; it's the landings that are different. For the three jump, the take-off and landing are on the same foot, whereas for the waltz jump, the feet change from take-off to landing. All you do is take off on the left foot on a forward outside edge, swing your right foot and leg in front (just like the Bunny Hop), turn half a rotation and land on the right back outside edge, with the left free leg stretched out behind the landing foot. Done!

Half Flip

This jump is a cute one with lots of possibilities to build on.

Throughout the book I've tried to make the point that once you learn the basics, all the fancy stuff can simply be added on to what you've already learned. One of the best examples of this is the half flip. Let's learn how to do it first and then I'll show you some of the things you can do from there.

STEP ONE

Starting with a right forward inside mohawk on a curve, turn from front to back, right foot to left. To keep yourself from rushing the take-off and jumping too soon, keep your right arm back and your left arm in front. Using the technique you've perfected from the back toe jump, stretch the right leg behind and firmly place your pick in the ice (1). Remember the "vault" feeling by stepping with your full weight over the toe pick as you jump.

STEP TWO

Instead of staying backward in the air, this time I want you to gently release your shoulder position to turn half a rotation (2) CCW to your left landing forward. Make your touch down with a quick left toe pick (3) and push on to the right forward inside edge (4) with the same kind of "peg leg" action you learned landing the bunny hop. For more control on the landing, put the left arm in front (5).

1 2 3 4 5

If the rhythm of the jump is giving you some trouble, practice walking through it first without jumping, just working on where the feet have to go. Do a tiny mohawk, step back on the right toe pick, step forward on the left toe and push on to the right forward inside edge. All you have to do now is add the jumping part between the right and left toe picks.

With some success on the half flip, let's talk variations.

Have you heard about the split jump and the stag jump? These are both glorified half flips.

Salchow

The next six jumps are the beginner single rotation jumps that all the double, triple and quadruple jumps are based on. Being able to *do* the singles will feel wonderful... but there's an added incentive—understanding how to perform them will help you identify the jumps when you're watching competitions on television. Bonus!

Simply put, these six basic jumps are defined at the take-off by three things: the direction of movement on the take-off (either forward or backward), the edge being skated (inside or outside) and the use of the toe pick (yes or no). Except for the number of rotations in the air (single, double, triple, etc.), once a jump is in flight they're all exactly the same. Every time a skater tries a different combination of these three things, it creates a different feeling to control, some easier and some more difficult, as you will find out.

BACKGROUND

The Sal, as skaters call the Salchow, is considered the easiest of the big jumps and is the first full rotation jump learned by beginners. The Sal is an edge jump (no toe pick is used) and takes off from a backward direction on an inside edge.

Preparation for the Sal can be tricky, not because it's such a hard jump, but because the natural action is quick and unexpected. The first time you attempt one, you'll be amazed at the power that comes from the edge as you wind up for the take-off. This kind of power will practically do the jump for you; all you have to do is hang on and make sure your body is in the right position.

STEP ONE

The standard approach is off a left forward outside three, turning to a left back inside edge for the actual take-off. Keeping the arms and shoulders in neutral at

your sides and the right free leg behind, hold that position for a couple of seconds, all the while increasing the bend in your skating knee (1).

STEP TWO

When you're ready to jump, swing the right free leg in an arc around the right side of your body (2) from behind to directly in front, a movement that signals the skating knee that it's time to spring into the air (3).

General Notes

To accomplish a good Salchow, use the toe picks sparingly; otherwise they'll act like brakes and destroy your speed. And another thing: Keeping your body checklist in mind will stop new problems from developing. You don't have to crank yourself around the jump to get the rotation done. That's the neat thing about singles; the curve of your pattern on the ice will give you all the rotation you need. Just relax and let it happen.

Step Three

Once you're up in the air, pretend you're doing a waltz jump (4) (5) (6) and land on the right back outside edge (7) (8).

Toe Loop

The Salchow may be the easiest edge jump in skating but it's the toe loop, or more commonly the "toe," that's considered the easiest toe jump.

Toe Loop

The toe loop has quite a wonderful history. I'll bet you didn't know that in some parts of the world it's called a "cherry flip" to give it more distinction from it's big sister, "the loop." It is also *the* jump in the march toward quadruple jumps; the quadruple toe is the most common quadruple done in competition to date.

The Best Jump

A little note is necessary here. For each of the jump elements, I'm presenting the most common entrances, but there are tons of other possibilities. For instance, another toe loop entry could be from a left forward outside three, changing feet to the right back outside edge to jump. The most important thing to remember is to be on the back outside edge for the take-off. Whether you use a three turn, a mohawk, or whatever, just get there the way that works best for you and gives you the best jump.

STEP ONE

Think back to when you first learned the right forward inside three and let's bring that old chestnut out to prepare for the toe loop. The forward inside three is the perfect preparation because it begins the rotational feeling and, more importantly, gets you neatly on the right back outside edge of the take-off without a lot of fuss (1). Those two words—back and outside—answer two of the questions about what defines the toe loop.

STEP TWO

Once you've turned the three, the next movement is to place the left toe pick in the ice, (2) repeating the same action you learned in the back toe jump. Transfer your weight quickly on to the toe pick using the left leg like a pole vault and kick your right foot and leg around to the left as if you were doing a waltz jump. (See how all the jumps are related?)

STEP THREE

Split the legs in the air and let your whole body rotate so your weight moves from the left toe pick to the right foot (3) (4) to prepare for landing on the right back outside edge (5) (6).

GENERAL NOTES

The toe is a great jump to have in your repertoire. Not only is it important as a jump on its own but it's hugely popular as part of a "combination" or "sequence," a succession of two or more jumps done in rapid succession.

Loop

1 2 3 4 5 6

BACKGROUND

If you ever get really serious about skating and progress beyond the single jumps, you'll want to have the loop jump "in your pocket"; that's skating lingo for a jump you do so well, you can always count on it working, even if your blade falls off.

Why is it so important?

In the air, the "feeling" of the loop jump is the basis for the body's posture, balance and action in all single and multi-rotational jumps from here on. To explain further, every other jump is unique only in its take-off; it then evolves into the loop once in flight or, to put it another way, some special move-ment is added to the beginning of the loop to give every other jump its own identity. Once you learn this loop feeling and can relate it to the other jumps, everything starts to make a huge amount of sense. Instead of thinking that every jump relies on a different set of techniques, you'll begin to see how closely related the jumps really are; for instance, the toe loop is just a loop jump with the toe pick used on take-off.

What sets the loop apart from other jumps is its simplicity. The take-off and landing are skated on the same foot and edge—right back outside—and because it's an edge jump, you never have to use the toe pick.

STEP ONE

Like the toe loop, start the take-off action with the same right forward inside three.

This time, once you've turned backward (1), instead of swinging the left leg behind to pick, like in the toe loop, leave it in front, slightly bent, and cross it over the

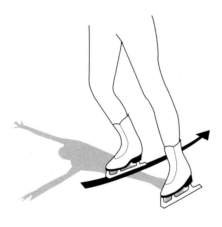

skating leg (2). At this point, with your left foot lifted off the ice, your balance may feel a bit "iffy," but to fully sense the loop action, you need all of your weight centered over the right foot (3). Trust me on this one.

STEP TWO

Make sure your right knee is nicely bent and spring into the air by straightening the skating knee and pressing forward on the blade. Start the rotation with the shoulders (3), letting the body follow along, but beware! The temptation to swing the left leg around will be huge. Don't let it happen! It will open the jump up and stop the rotation, causing the body to feel scattered and messy, as if you have nothing firm to hang on to.

STEP THREE

When you do win the left-leg-battle, turn once in the air (4), landing on the same right back outside edge as the take-off. On the landing, let the left leg uncross and move behind to landing position (5).

Welcome to the world of the loop jump. Now that you have that one in your pocket, we can really get moving.

Flip

The next bouncer on the family tree of jumps is another toe jump called the flip.

BACKGROUND

Once you review its method, you'll see the flip is related to other single rotation jumps in two major ways. First, its preparation is exactly like the Salchow with a toe pick added (in fact, some people call the flip a toe Salchow), and secondly, once the toe pick makes its stab in the ice, the nature of the jump changes to a loop.

Flip Rules

Don't confuse the flip with the "back flip," the on-ice and in-the-air version of a backward circus somersault. That flip is not considered acceptable in amateur competition due to its acrobatic nature and the fact it's usually landed on two feet. Oh, we tried it for a while—back in the 70s and 80s the back flip became quite the thing until the International Skating Union (the worldwide governing body of figure skating) finally put its foot ... or, um, blade ... down, and ruled it illegal. Today, however, it's still a big part of skating and fairly common in exhibitions and shows.

The direction of the take-off is backward and from the left back inside edge, the same as the Sal, although the shape of the entry is somewhat straighter in the flip to give the toe pick a better chance to find its proper placement. Too much curl on the three and the pick will hit the ice too far to the side of the body rather than directly behind, a move that stops the jump's momentum across the ice. It won't "go" anywhere and therefore looks more like a hiccup.

In terms of the flip's action on the take-off, there are some more obvious differences from the Sal, too.

On the Sal, if you recall, before jumping you pause for a moment after the left forward outside three turn. On the flip, the timing is much quicker. The toe pick plants firmly in the ice as soon as you turn backward. Unlike the Sal, where the weight is on the left foot at take-off, in the flip the take-off is actually from the toe of the right picking foot—à la loop jump.

Step One

Set up your left forward outside three (1), a little straighter than the one you used for your Sal. As you turn backward and get ready to pick, have your left arm in front and your right arm behind.

Step Two

With your left knee bent, reach behind with your right leg and, keeping it fairly straight, poke the right toe into the ice (2). As you pull your legs together, left foot crossed over the right, quickly move your balance to the right toe pick (3). Don't begin the rotation until you've made that weight change.

Step Three

For a fraction of a second before jumping, you should be standing over the right toe pick with the left foot crossed in front of the lower right leg (4) (at the top of your right boot). Now you're in the perfect position to jump. Spring off a slightly bent right knee, turn one full rotation (5) and land on a right back outside edge. The toe pick and landing are on the same foot (6).

Lutz

This jump is one tough cookie.

In terms of the three defining characteristics, the Lutz is almost identical to the flip—the entry is backward and uses the same toe pick. The only difference from the flip, and it's a big one, is that the Lutz take-off is skated on a left back outside edge, whereas the flip uses a left back inside. Also like the flip, the Lutz is closely related to the loop because of the action the skater must feel once the weight is transferred over the toe pick on take-off. You wouldn't think that one little difference, back outside vs. back inside, would have such an enormous effect on the difficulty of the jump, but it's that tiny change of balance that makes the Lutz such a beast. It's all about curves.

BACKGROUND

With every jump up to this point, you have skated CCW to jump CCW, forming a pattern on the ice like one giant arc. To prepare for the left back outside take-off of the Lutz, the setup is reverse (CW) and makes the completed shape of the Lutz like a backward "S" with two arcs joined at the middle. The first arc of the "S" is the shape skated up to and including the toe pick, and the second arc is the path the body takes in the air and on the landing. The skater makes a wide backward CW curve approaching the take-off, picks the toe into the ice, and then must reverse direction to rotate in the standard CCW fashion. To put it simply, you just get going one way on the take-off, then you have to turn around and jump in the other direction. See what I mean?

When the Lutz is first taught, many beginners think they have to learn to jump and rotate opposite to their natural feeling. Let me put those fears to rest. Although some skaters do have some fun trying to jump in the opposite direction, that's not what the Lutz is all about. It's just the preparation we're talking about here, OK?

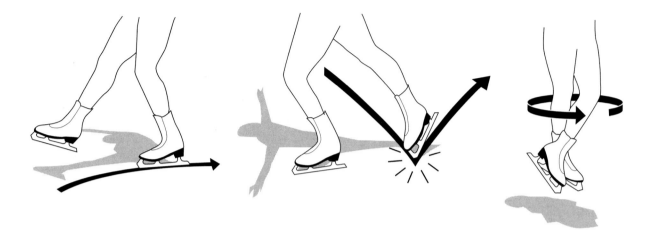

STEP ONE

Give it a try by skating backward CW crosscuts, your right foot crossing over the left. When you're comfy, push on to a gentle left back outside edge, holding your left arm in front and your right arm behind. Look over your right shoulder if you like, gliding with your right free foot and leg stretched slightly out in front and in line with your skating foot.

STEP TWO

When you bring your head back around to face forward and you feel ready to pick, bend the skating knee and reach behind with the right toe pick to tap into the ice. This is the tricky moment when you've finished skating the top curve of the "S" and started forming the bottom and opposite arc.

STEP THREE

Although you'll feel the tendency to continue moving CW, remember this is the puzzle of the Lutz. To solve it, climb over the right toe pick and do an ordinary loop jump.

It will likely take more than a few tries to get this one sorted out . . . but it's worth it.

Lutz Overview

The Lutz is recognizable by its long diagonal entry (2 and 3) and its S-shaped pattern when completed. The left back outside edge at the moment of the pick (4) means the skater must enter in a clockwise direction (1–4), then rotate counterclockwise (5–9) in the opposite direction. The Lutz is called a counter-rotation jump, and the counterrotation significantly increases the difficulty.

Chapter 5
Basic Spins

Two-Foot Spin

The most important factors affecting your ability to spin are your balance, your technique, your body type and your strength. When you get into tougher spins, like a camel spin, your fitness level and flexibility will become significant, too.

BACKGROUND

Most spins begin as backward crosscuts. We're going to start before that—to get you spinning on a spot without having to control a lot of speed from the preparation. This will give you a taste of spinning without making you too dizzy.

STEP ONE

To begin, make sure you're standing perfectly erect, back straight, head facing forward, butt tucked beneath you, feet together. Staying in one spot, try walking around yourself in tiny circles with your arms out to the side at waist level. Now, without stopping turning, stand on two feet with your weight equally distributed, and see if you can keep spinning, even for a short time. That's the feeling we're going for!

STEP TWO

Now I want you to pretend you're holding a beach ball out in front of your chest. If your natural spinning direction is CW (to the right), start the beach ball off to your left side, with your upper body facing to the left. Balanced on your left foot with your right toe pick in the ice and feet shoulder-width apart, throw the imaginary ball to the right. When you throw the "ball," push gently with your left foot and move your weight on to the

right blade, keeping your right knee slightly bent. As you start to spin, try to bring your feet close together (almost pigeon-toed) until you feel comfortable enough to balance on both feet. Once you've released your "ball," most skaters like to bring their arms in close to the body, hands clasped together in front near the waist, and elbows tucked in. If you managed even one full rotation, good stuff!

STEP THREE

Here's where we should talk about dizziness. In the early stages of learning to spin, you'll probably feel like your eyeballs won't stay still. To counter those

reactions, you may resort to all sorts of strange movements, such as closing your eyes, or "spotting," like when a ballet dancer turns her head faster than her body to concentrate on one particular point on the horizon. In skating we just let nature takes its course. You will feel dizzy, but over time as your technique improves, your dizziness will disappear.

STEP FOUR

Keep working, concentrate on keeping the body straight and balanced...and stay away from your toe picks. The perfect spot on your blade to be balanced on is just behind the toe picks, slightly kissing the bottom pick to keep your balance but not so far up on them that they act like a set of emergency brakes. To keep spinning as long as possible, you don't want any friction.

STEP FIVE

When a spin is well done, friction will almost disappear. The spin will seem to go on forever, rotating quickly and centering in one spot on the ice. Although any spin will have a unique sound of repeating "shhooms" as the blade moves in tiny circles, it shouldn't sound overly scratchy. Above all, work on your body

line—stretched and compact, with an eye for a beautifully simple position.

One-Foot Spin

The Layback—one type of one-foot spin.

After the two-foot spin, spinning on one foot will be a piece of cake. You've already learned the hardest part—how to rotate quickly over a long period of time.

BACKGROUND

We're going to accomplish two things in this lesson: first, how to make the transition from balancing on two feet to one; and second, how to spruce up the spin by wrapping it in an attractive entrance and exit.

Shifting your balance from two feet to one in a spin is as simple as gliding on two feet in a straight line and lifting up one foot. If your posture is good in a spin, it's definitely easier. When you're spinning, the forces are stronger than when you're moving in a straight line, a fact that makes an average spin even better, but a poor spin . . . well, let's not go there.

The thing to remember in a spin is to move gently so as to avoid destroying the balance and form.

The slightest change of position can have disastrous results on the quality of the spin, but if you concentrate on keeping the action smooth and circular, theoretically you will be able to wrap your free foot around your head and still stay spinning.

Theories are great, but right now you need to know how to make this one-foot thing happen.

STEP ONE

Start a regular two-foot spin that feels like it's got some life to it (speed and duration) and gradually lift the right foot off the ice. Since you should be spinning with both feet close together, the right foot won't have far to go. At first, lift it only slightly off the ice, keeping it touching the left spinning foot. When you have repeated that action enough to believe in yourself, lift the right foot up higher and place it against the inside calf of your left leg (5) almost at knee level. For the best balance, keep the bent right knee pointing straight in front so that if someone was

watching your spin from the side, it would look like the number "4." You'll eventually notice that you're spinning on a back inside edge.

STEP TWO

Now the fun part: how to enter and exit. Every basic spin begins and ends the same way. To enter, wind up for the spin by skating left backward crosscuts (CW) and ending the crosscuts with a deep right back inside edge (1) (RBI). Holding the RBI, let the left arm come in front and the right arm behind (2). From here, plan on stepping forward on a left outside edge by bending the left knee and bringing the shoulders around. Curve the LFO (left forward outside edge) deeply into the center of the circle and, to start the rotation, swing the right free leg around the body from behind to in front (3). Let the left knee straighten as you three turn from left forward outside to left back inside (4).

Step Three

If you want to speed up your rotation, bring the arms in close to the body; if you want to slow down, open the arms away from the body. Any increase in your speed will tempt you to rock too far forward on the blade. In spinning, the toe picks are asked to do a lot to help you stay balanced. Just beware: too much toe can slow you down or spin you completely out of control, too little can cause you to tip off your heel. Aim to balance on the spot on your blade just behind the picks.

Step Four

The most common exit for spins is like the landing of jumps, on a right back outside edge. As the spin slows down but before it dies completely, push on to a right back outside edge away from the center (6).

As we move into spins with more challenging positions, use this entrance and exit, always starting and ending the rotation like an ordinary one-foot spin.

Corkscrew

The corkscrew is nothing but a fancy one-foot spin. The spin is very fast and, with the characteristic leg position, it has a barber pole effect that is easy to recognize.

A Clockwise Corkscrew

STEP ONE

After the ordinary wind-up and entry, step on a deep LFO (left forward outside) edge with a softly bent knee. Bring your right free leg in front by swinging it around the body, all the while keeping your shoulders and arms in neutral position facing forward over your left foot.

Don't rush. Take a few revolutions to find your balance. This is the point on your blade over which you must stay no matter what you do with the rest of the body. When you find it, hang on!

STEP TWO

To increase the speed of the spin, do two things at once: clasp your hands together in front of your chest as if you are hugging a tree, and bend your right knee, bringing your right foot to a position resting slightly above your skating knee. Slowly pull the hands in toward the body until your arms are straight, at the same time push the right foot down the skating leg until your ankles are crossed. If you've managed to hold on, you are now a blur!

STEP THREE

Every movement you do that makes your body tighter and more compact will speed up a spin. As it gets faster, the force pulling your arms and legs away from the center of your body will also get more powerful to the point where it will take every bit of strength you have to keep the spin under control. (Competitors often worry about their nose running if they have a corkscrew at the end of their program—I don't think we need any further explanation on that one.)

As well as being a spin in its own right, the corkscrew is usually skated as a final position for all other spins.

Camel Spin

Someone once told me a perfectly silly but believable reason for the camel spin's name. When skaters are learning it, their hip and back positions are so ugly, they look like camels. The truth is I don't really know where the camel name originated, but I do know I've seen more than a few humps watching skaters struggle to control this difficult position. Yet, when it's done well, the camel is one of the most exquisitely beautiful spins in skating.

STEP ONE

By now, you should be an expert on the preparation for any spin (1) (2), so let's throw you a wrinkle on the camel entry. Instead of bringing your right leg around in front as you curve on the LFO, leave it directly behind you (3).

STEP TWO

When you turn your "3" to begin the spin, bend your upper body forward from the waist (think of pointing your belly button at the ice surface) (4).

1   2   3   4

STEP THREE

At the same moment, with a teeter-totter action, lift your right leg up in the air behind you into a "spiral" position. The bodyline from the tip of your right toe to the top of your head should be parallel to the ice, arms extended out to the side at shoulder level.

STEP FOUR

S-T-R-E-T-C-H. (To be successful, the camel position will always require a little extra work.)

STEP FIVE

Like the entry, the exit to the camel is a bit odd. From the spiraling position, the right leg must drop down and swing around in front, as the upper body stands upright. It's at this stage that many fine camels fall apart because the change in posture and balance is so dramatic. "Forewarned is forearmed," they say. Be prepared for it by concentrating on your balance point. Let the body make its move by focusing on staying centered, then it's a simple matter of completing the element with a one-foot spin and pushing on to the normal RBO (right back outside) edge to exit.

GENERAL NOTES

You may be one of those lucky people who find the camel easy. If you are, experiment with some variations in your positions, either with your arms or with your upper body. Look around you. You'll see camels where the arms are held tightly against the body or where the upper body is turned nearly upside down.

What works best for you depends on which position gives you the best spin. Try them all and, if you want to, invent some of your own.

Sit Spin

Have you ever heard the term "shoot-the-duck"? It's skating lingo for a move learned by beginners that involves crouching down on one foot and gliding in a straight line with the other foot stretched out in front, "taking aim." This position forms the basic posture in the sit spin.

STEP ONE

Start your entry like a one-foot spin but bring your right leg around and in front with more force and in a wider circle (1).

STEP TWO

As your right leg is making its move, bend your left skating knee so deeply that your whole body crouches down to the point where your derrière is only inches from the ice (2).

STEP THREE

Once you reach your sit, the right free leg, the one doing the "shoot-the-duck," should be held in front almost parallel to the ice, with the foot close to the ice and the toe turned out (3).

1

2

3

GENERAL NOTES

The position of the free leg is really optional. Depending on your personal technique and body type, you may find you're most comfortable in a very low position with the right leg held out perfectly straight. Others may prefer a spin that is not as low to the ice, where the right leg is bent and slightly curled around the skating foot. Both styles are beautiful.

Whether your leg is bent or straight, avoid spinning with the knees together. First of all, it's terribly uncomfortable, and secondly, it makes the small circles you're tracing tinier and more impossible to control. Your spin will go bonkers.

Where you put your arms will also affect how deeply you sit in the spin. When skaters are learning the sit spin, they often try to help themselves balance by leaning on the skating knee. Put a spell on that one; not only is it unattractive, it actually gets in the way of finding the best overall spinning position. The most useful option is to place your arms in front, one hand on top of the other, in a line running down the right leg, stretched toward the right foot. This will help find the correct level for you—a depth in the knee that is low enough so that you can easily hold the position, but not so low that, your butt is brushing the ice.

Although I've been a nag about posture and keeping your back erect, the sit spin is a legal opportunity to break the rules; in fact, during the spin, I want you to. With your whole upper body, bend forward from the hips, but keep your back straight as you do it. Don't curl your spine or slouch your shoulders. This aspect of the spin is crucial for balance. To offset the force of the leg being held out in front, the back must lean forward.

On your first few attempts, you may feel the urge to put your right foot down to help you get back upright to complete the one-foot spin and the RBO exit. OK. But if your spin has been a fairly good one and you still have some momentum, the strength in your left leg will be able to handle standing back up on one foot.

Back Spin

Just to confuse you, when you refer to spinning "backward" or "forward," it has absolutely nothing to do with your direction of movement.

If you're talking about direction, all spins are skated on backward edges with the heel of the skating foot leading the circle. So what's the deal?

BACKGROUND

When referring to spins, the terms "forward" and "backward" tell you what foot the skater is on. For CCW, forward spins are done on the left foot and backward spins are done on the right.

A good spin defies gravity by overcoming friction over a long period of time. (Some skaters have been timed doing one spin that lasted for several minutes!) To do this, the goal of a spinner is to rotate on a "flat," that point on the blade where there is the least resistance. For most of us, however, the reality is a little different and we make a few compromises by spinning as close to the "flat" as possible, making tiny backward circles. For a forward spin, skate on a slight back inside edge on the left foot; for a backward spin, skate on a slight back outside edge on the right.

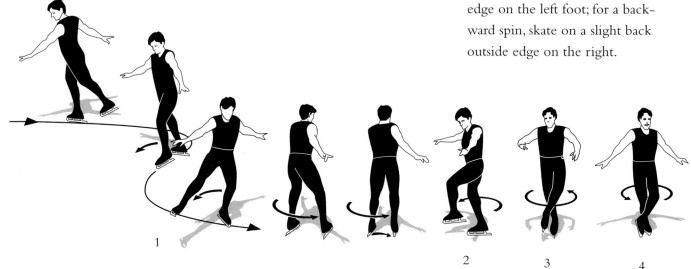

1

2

3

4

The spins you have been working on up 'til now have all been forward spins, skated on the left foot and tracing back inside circles.

What happens if you wind up to perform a standard two-foot spin (1) and instead of lifting the right foot to make it a one-foot spin, you lift the left (2)? Do you feel some confusion about which edge to use on the right foot? Where do you put the left free leg once it's raised off the ice? Does the upright body position threaten to collapse? These are all good questions.

STEP ONE

Before trying the back spin again, the most important thing to figure out is that the spin must be done on the right back outside edge—like the backward half of a right forward inside three. In order to get on the RBO, you'll need to cross the left foot and leg in front over the right (3) and once again, as in the corkscrew, you'll get a dramatic barber pole effect, only

faster. With a firm RBO edge and the correct position of the left free leg, the tendency for the body to break at the waist will be completely eliminated (4). You'll have a wonderfully natural feeling that could go on forever. This spin is also called a back scratch spin and when you hear and feel the toe picks in action, you'll understand why.

STEP TWO

You have two major choices for the exit. The easiest but definitely not the most fun is to simply put your left foot down on the ice, change feet to return to a normal one-foot spin and push out on a RBO edge. Far more challenging is to unwrap the left leg, moving it in a giant arc back around and away from the right leg. It's the same RBO edge as usual only this time, the right foot must propel itself out of the spin without any help from the left foot. Give it a whirl.

GENERAL NOTES

Before you rush into more complicated back spins in either the camel or sit positions, I recommend you really fine-tune the basic back scratch. Being able to perform one without thinking will free up the brainpower you're going to need when you tackle other variations.

Chapter 6
Field Moves

Spiral

The spiral is a simple move done gliding forward or backward on one foot, either in a straight line or on a curve, with the other leg held behind in a high arabesque. It may indeed be simple, but you know, after all my years in skating, a good spiral performed to beautiful music can still give me the shivers.

Average spirals are a dime a dozen, but an exquisite spiral takes as much effort and practice as any triple jump—there are very few.

BACKGROUND

In any field move, the position should be held for a long period of time and should be overflowing with expression and artistry. That doesn't necessarily mean the element should be busy or "gucked up" with changes and arm movements (some of the most beautiful spirals are very plain), but it does require the body to be perfectly in line and stretched to its full potential.

You might consider this bad news but getting the body in shape for learning a spiral takes a bit of preparation and conditioning. You can try to do it quickly or suddenly but if you value walking without pain, I'd advise taking it slowly.

STEP ONE

Begin by holding on at the boards or work on it at home in front of a mirror. Start gently.

Although spirals need to be done on both feet, at first choose the leg that feels the most comfortable to stand on (if you jump CCW, that's probably your right leg), stretch your left leg behind and point your toe. Slowly lift your left leg directly behind your body and without twisting or bending the body forward, raise the leg as far as you can. When it's reached its limit, carefully lower your upper body. This should allow you to lift the leg even further. Keep the leg straight and pointed. And make sure you only continue bending the body forward if the leg is still rising.

STEP TWO

Finally the leg will hit a point where the muscles will not stretch any further without a lot of pain. That's fine. Stop and hold it there for a few seconds, then, as you raise the body, let the foot settle back to the floor. Try it again just like a teeter-totter, treating the upper body and the spiraling leg like one complete slab; don't raise or lower one without lowering and raising the other.

STEP THREE

With each repeated attempt, the action will feel smoother and easier and you may even sense the leg is getting slightly higher. Gradually your muscles will feel looser. Yippee! That's the whole idea—improvement by intelligent repetition.

STEP FOUR

Now what about the back? The key to doing a great spiral is arching the back. To get the perfect arch, you have to be aware of several things. First of all, lowering your body will not necessarily heighten your leg and foot; the muscles in the groin and buttocks do most of that work and therefore must be trained and coaxed to be flexible. It all takes time and patience . . . and doing it over and over again . . . and on both feet.

GENERAL NOTES

At first you will feel enormous strain on your back, but if you lift your head and shoulders up, letting the rest of your back stay relatively flat, the spiral picture will look much more pleasing.

Unfortunately, many skaters think all they need to do for a spiral is to have their leg up in the air for a second or two; the position is never sustained. Their bodies are loose and gangly, their free leg is bent, and generally the

move has the look of an unmade bed. With some daily commitment to getting flexible, your position will improve quickly and so will your control. Don't worry about whether your leg ever hits the heavens; strive for a stretched and satisfying position that feels beautiful to you.

Shoot-the-Duck

You've already had a brief intro-duction to the shoot-the-duck in the lesson on sit spins. My job is to encourage you. Although you may get snowy and wet, the shoot-the-duck is an important element for learning even more about balance and position. Think of it this way. Once you've crouched down, you won't have far to go if you fall.

STEP ONE

The best way to get warmed up for the shoot-the-duck is to try it on two feet first. With some decent speed under your belt (you know how everything is easier if you're traveling at a good clip), lean forward and bend your knees while gliding on both feet in a straight line.

Lower your whole body until your bottom is resting on the heels of your skates. Put your arms slightly out in front or clasp your knees if it feels natural.

STEP TWO

Completely bending your knees without falling may seem impossible at this stage. You need to bend carefully to stay balanced but after the first part of the descent, you'll feel "stuck"— either unable to bend your knees further or unable to stay where you are. This is "the point of no return." If you stay at that first level, you haven't accomplished a successful shoot-the-duck position; if you force yourself to continue bending, you can't stop until you're all the way down. Go the whole route. Surprisingly, when you hit the lowest level, it's actually comfortable. Practice the bend and the crouch on two feet until you feel you have it mastered.

STEP THREE

Skating the shoot-the-duck on one foot isn't much different. Naturally the balance is a little harder and instead of your weight being distributed between two legs, now one leg must do all the work.

Let's suppose it's your left leg. Prepare the same way as for a two-foot shoot-the-duck but before bending, move all your weight over to glide on the left foot. Bending forward, stretch the right foot and leg straight out in front of the left and keep your right foot fairly close to the ice. Don't hang on to the right leg, it can manage on its own. Concentrate on your balance.

STEP FOUR

By now you should be able to lower yourself quite quickly into the full sitting position, this time with the right foot and leg "aimed" out in front. Sure, once you're all the way down, you can hang on to the right leg if it needs a little support, but don't pull on it if you do. That will cause it to lift too high off the ice and rock you back on your heel (you'll end up sliding on your back with your right foot "aimed" at the ceiling). Many skaters place their left hand and lower arm on the left knee or in any position that allows the move to glide forever.

STEP FIVE

To get out of the shoot-the-duck, run the entire process in reverse. In a perfect world, straightening the knee should happen while still gliding on one foot. Work toward that goal but for now, if you need to put the right foot back down on the ice to help you stand back up, it'll be your secret.

GENERAL NOTES

If you skate a few shoot-the-ducks, you're bound to notice the muscle in the left leg feeling a bit tender. If you don't overdo it, the soreness will pass quickly as the body adapts.

The best fitness strategy is to practice small amounts of all of the elements each day you skate. The more frequently you can skate, perhaps two or three times a week, the faster your progress will be.

Spread Eagle

An Ina Bauer is a stylized Spread Eagle

This movement is one of the few elements in skating where gliding on two feet is a good thing.

As a viewer and a fan you may not know the name of this position. You can easily recognize the spread eagle, though, because of the turned out position of both feet and both legs—they are spread like an eagle's wings.

BACKGROUND

Some skaters take to the spread eagle easily, those with natural flexibility in their hips. Others, like me, have to grind away at teaching the body and feet exactly where to go. Don't let anyone tell you it's impossible if you're not built the right way. If I can do it, anyone can. People like us just have to train a little harder.

There are two types of spread eagles: inside and outside. Not only is the inside spread eagle much easier, it's also a great stepping stone in training for the outside; all the same muscles are used only to a lesser degree.

What makes an inside or outside spread eagle? Simple. It's the edges you glide on. The inside spread eagle is typically slower and skated on a smaller circle; the outside spread eagle is the larger and faster big brother.

Right now it's the inside spread eagle for us.

STEP ONE

To get a sense of the position for your feet, stand on the floor without your skates on and spread your feet about a shoulder's width apart. Stand right up over top of them with your knees straight and see how far

you can turn your toes out, a bit at a time. The more, the better. Hang on to a chair if you need some support, but never twist your feet to the point of pain. After all, this exercise is not supposed to be torture. All I want you to discover is the basic feeling and the idea of how much stretching and flexing you're going to have to do before the spread eagle can become a reality on the rink.

STEP TWO

Try the same exercise on the ice with your skates on. Hold yourself at the boards with your feet apart and place them so your heels face each other and your toes turn out to the side. Stand with your weight evenly distributed and balanced on each blade at a point just ahead of the heel. Push your hips in close to the boards so you won't be tempted to bend forward.

STEP THREE

When you can hold your feet in that position without too much effort, see what happens when you pull yourself slowly in one direction along the boards. Do you find it easier to hold the position when you're moving? Even if you travel only a few inches, congratulations, you've done your first spread eagle!

STEP FOUR

Now it's time to test your skill away from the boards.

Stroke slowly in a CCW direction and prepare to glide on a circle on a right forward inside edge. After pushing with the left foot, swing the left leg in front of the right and then, as you let it swing back again, turn your left toe out for the spread eagle position. Place it on the ice on a backward inside edge half a meter or so behind the right (which is on a forward inside edge), on the same circle shape. Balance equally on both feet. Remember: don't bend your knees. Think about pushing your hips strongly toward the center of the circle and arching your back.

GENERAL NOTES

The hardest part about the spread eagle is having the strength and control to keep your toes turned out, an ability that improves with time. As you enjoy the inside spread eagle position, play with variations in your arm positions and with your speed until, finally, you're ready to tackle the more demanding outside spread eagle. Work up to it in the same way and soon you'll be able to add it to your repertoire.

Pivot

BACKGROUND

The pivot is the "bull's eye" of figure skating—a one-foot edge in the shape of a small circle with the toe of one foot picking in the ice at the center of the bull's eye and the other foot gliding around the rim of the circle.

There are many variations of this field move, inside and outside, backward and forward. All can be used either as moves on their own, highlighting music and choreography, or as movements accenting the endings of jumps or spins.

Step One Step Two Step Three Step Four

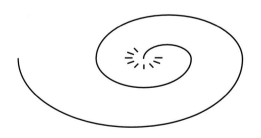

Illustration of Pattern

STEP ONE

One of the hardest pivots is the back outside skated on a right back outside edge (RBO). With this pivot, because of its backward direction, you won't be able to see the center of the bull's eye as your foot reaches behind to pick. This can make things a little tough.

STEP TWO

Glide CCW on a RBO and reach behind you with a bent left leg. You won't find the center with your left toe pick right away, so let the toe drag on the ice for several seconds (it will make a scratchy sound) until you connect. The back outside edge will feel more comfortable if you use lots of knee bend. When you find the center, let most of your weight rest on the toe pick once you feel secure.

STEP THREE

The more control and speed you have, the longer you'll be able to glide in the position, but if you can get one full rotation without stopping at first, that's pretty good.

GENERAL NOTES

All pivots have the same characteristics: a toe pick at the center of the bull's eye, with the other foot gliding around it on the circumference of the circle.

Footwork

BACKGROUND

Footwork is a term used to describe any series of steps, turns, hops and edges. It may be used to connect all other elements or as an element on its own (it's so important, it's a "required element" in competition). Any footwork sequence is composed of basic moves from figures, free skating and dance that are combined in a variety of unique ways.

Believe it or not, you can already do many of these skating tid-bits to make up your own footwork, and when you study further on into dance, you'll know even more. Use things like crosscuts, three turns, spirals, small jumps one rotation or less, mohawks, spread eagles, etc., to design your sequence.

Although doing your footwork to music is not absolutely essential, it will likely help the creative process. Listen and let the music tell you what to do. If you prefer to work on your sequence silently at first, that's great too, but plan for the future to find a piece of music that makes your feet "bop," and design a step that fits it. After all, skating to music is what the sport is all about.

When you're ready to choreo-
graph, there are several things to
consider.

- Which steps do you want to
  use?

- What order will you put them
  in?

- What kind of pattern do you
  want to skate on the ice—
  straight line, circular or "S"-
  shaped?

- Plan to use different directions
  of rotation—CW and CCW.

- Skate your footwork at vari-
  ous speeds—fast and slow.

- Emphasize the movement
  with unique arm and body
  positions.

- Experiment with the body at
  different levels—crouches and
  leaps are also important to
  include.

GENERAL NOTES

If you feel overwhelmed with
the task, start with just a few
steps and then play "add-on," a
game skaters use to test their
memories by adding on a new
step every time they repeat the
sequence. Being able to think
quickly and recall steps with
confidence is a talent that takes
practice, just like the steps themselves.

A technique that works very well
to help your memory is to write
down your steps in order in a
notebook. This allows you to do
some homework off the ice—sit
quietly and review your steps.

Design your steps slowly at first
and don't settle for the easy stuff.
Once your steps are cemented in
your mind and you've mastered
them while going slowly, press
on the accelerator a notch and
try it faster. And then faster again
until you can't increase your
speed any further.

Challenge yourself. You'll rise to
the occasion.

Chapter 7
Dance

Progressives

Care to dance?

Now is when you get a chance
to put into use the results of all
those hours you've been practicing your forward stroking by
stringing several steps together
into one of the basic dance steps
called a "progressive."

BACKGROUND

In dance, you'll use all the same principles you've learned for good forward skating—concentrating on your posture: back straight, knees bent, head erect and facing forward, arms out to the side at waist level. And, when learning any new move, start slowly and patiently. Don't rush. It only makes things more difficult.

A progressive is a series of three steps skated on a curve, all moving in one direction. The steps consist of three edges pushed in succession, usually an outside edge first, then an inside, then an outside again. If you're traveling in a counter-clockwise direction (CCW), moving to your left, it's called a left progressive because it starts by stepping on the left foot first, then the right, then the left once more. In the clockwise direction (CW), the right foot is the first step of the right progressive.

STEP ONE

When you move onto the ice, begin the movement by gliding CCW. If you start the progressive on your left foot, do you notice that the first edge is on the outside? Staying on the same curve for the next step on the right will be an inside edge, and as you return for the third step on the left foot, once again you repeat the outside edge.

To summarize, a common progressive is a series of three edges: left outside, right inside and left outside going CCW. In the reverse CW direction, it's right outside, left inside and right outside.

STEP TWO

To build on your ease and confidence during the step, really work with every push to bring your feet completely together before pushing on to the next step. By practicing this way with what I call "neat feet," your balance and control will improve in leaps and bounds. If you're less fussy about the placement of your feet, you'll always feel slightly nervous about trusting your balance.

STEP THREE

At first, make each of the three steps equal in time and ice coverage as you move around the curve. Once you feel secure in both directions, try making an "S" pattern by skating a left progressive (CCW) and then following it with a right one (CW). In fact, why don't you see how many progressives you can put together in one continuous sequence by alternating left and right across the rink? It's like writing a whole bunch of connected "S's" on the ice.

Since dancing always means
music, now you can try to skate
those three steps of each progressive to a rhythm. For instance, in
the Dutch Waltz, one of the ele-
mentary dances, the whole progressive takes six beats of music.
Now, wouldn't it be easy if those
six beats were divided evenly
between the progressive's three
steps—two beats per step? Well,
we don't want to be easy, so
instead, skate with a kind of
"peg-leg" action that takes two
beats for the first step, one beat
for the second step, and three
beats for the third. Sometimes
just trying it to real music will
help you get the right feeling.

Now you can have some fun!
Once you start skating to music,
your life will never be the same.

Chasse

**Another common step in ice dancing is the
"chasse" (pronounced sha-say). The chasse is so
similar to the progressive, at first glance you may
not see the distinction. They are made up of the
same three steps, left-right-left, or right-left-right,
and the same types of edges, outside-inside-outside.
The difference is in the second step of the three-
step progression. In the progressive, the second step
pushes like the first and third, but in the chasse, this
is not the case. Rather than push, the second step
merely lifts off the ice beside the skating foot. In
still another step, the slide chasse, the second step
slides forward and stretches out in front.**

Swing Roll

BACKGROUND

Think back many pages to when you were first experimenting with one-foot gliding on the ice. When you try it now, I'll bet you can hardly recognize yourself.

Remember when you began attempting forward outside edges, those heavenly little arcs that curved around the hockey line, first on one side of the line and then on the other? If you've been serious about practicing them, by now you have shed the "beginner" and are ready to advance them to the next level—as swing rolls.

Chasse Position

STEP ONE

Take an ordinary left forward outside edge and make it grow. Give it more speed and skate it on a larger circle so it has more flow. Spice it up with some of that ballroom attitude you've been working on, with lots of bend in the skating knee and some good, strong edges.

STEP TWO

Finally, and this is the new part, after you push and extend the free leg fully behind you, swing the free leg completely in front until it stretches and points to its maximum. Make the movement of the free leg smooth and definite by keeping it as straight as possible.

Slide Chasse

As your leg swings forward, let the skating knee rise slightly, not so much it becomes stiff, but just enough to give yourself a little lift.

GENERAL NOTES

The swinging action of the free leg should look like the pendulum of a clock—equal time and distance behind and in front of the skating leg. As with any dance step, the quality of the feeling improves greatly when skated to music. Try it out by choosing music that does something to you. Although rock and rap might be your favorite for listening on the radio, medium speed classical selections are better for dancing on the ice, at least until you get a few more miles on those blades.

Add to those miles once you feel secure on the forward steps by flipping the steps over and trying them backwards. Three of the four steps turn around beautifully—progressive, chasse and swing roll—as a forward element; the slide chasse is the only holdout.

Dancing may become your major focus in learning to skate. Ice dancing has thrills of its own and requires many of the same skills as free skating: athleticism, artistry, flexibility, fitness, technical ability and control. As a matter of fact, I've often thought if free skaters were to study ice dancing, they would become better free skaters.

Graduation

Congratulations!

You've worked hard, paid attention and motivated yourself at times when a lot of other people would have stopped.

If you've fulfilled your desire to actively learn about figure skating, you've succeeded in a significant way. If there's still more "fueling" to be done to satisfy your skating appetite, that's wonderful, too. There's still lots to learn.

In the meantime, use your new knowledge. You've felt what it's like to test yourself—you've even launched yourself into the air when you didn't really know how to come down. You've learned a lot about your body and how it works. You've also trained your mind, to cope with failure . . . and success, to set goals and to understand what it takes to achieve them. Learning anything new, particularly when there is an element of danger, is no small feat.

Now it's time for a confession. My life has been blessed with the most unbelievable experiences, all as a result of figure skating, and, despite the fact there were a few medals involved, it's never been the medals that have given me the greatest gift. Skating has taught me lessons about life— some of those lessons have been harsh and painful but, you know what, I'd do it all over again if I had the choice.

Although skating may not become a major focus in your life, my wish for you is that you have fun with it. Relish learning something difficult. The only cost is patience . . . and time. You've proven to me that you have what it takes to make that kind of investment. Now you have the right to call yourself a figure skater.

Acknowledgements

In the same way that becoming a good skater requires teamwork, the writing of any book depends on the input and skills of many other people beyond the author.

Several years ago, a close friend and another skating writer, Steve Milton, was approached by Key Porter to do an instructional book. Because Steve considers himself an expert "observer" rather than an expert "skater," he declined the offer and sent the publisher looking in my direction. At that time, this was the book they wanted to do. Instead, I sold them on *The Spectator's Guide to Figure Skating*. This time around, they said, "We did what you wanted. Now it's your turn." Thanks to the energy and precision of my editor, Andrea Bock, we made it! (If I'm reading the signs correctly, I think she wants to learn to skate.)

The world of skating has been a blessing in my life. Right from my roots in Unionville, Ontario at the Unionville Skating Club through to my teaching career in Toronto at the North Toronto Skating Club, friends and colleagues have kindly shared their amazing resources.

Eric Anweiler, the Manager of the North Toronto Arena provided ice time to shoot many of the photographs.

Coach Lucy Kovac volunteered time with her talented students Kathleen Savage and Jamie Kyle.

Photographer Pete Patterson patiently clicked through infinite numbers of rolls of film looking for the perfect shot.

And I now consider illustrator John Lightfoot an honorary skater.

Thanks also to my wonderful family, Jill, Chris and Bruce who helped interpret skating lingo into everyday English.

Without fail, each one of these creative individuals instantly captured the spirit of this book and enthusiastically helped bring it to life.

Now let's have a skating party!

Index